CW00543108

Praise for *Nobody Lives Here*

'Lex's very detailed, vivid and moving account of his experience offers a deeply personal reflection on the Holocaust in the Netherlands. Readers will be captivated as he recalls the plight of his Jewish community in German-occupied Amsterdam, and how he managed to avoid the same fate. He shares how he, as a young boy, was forced into hiding, in multiple locations and on multiple occasions, sleeping in stairwells and trusting strangers – some of whom undoubtedly saved his life with their kindness. His bravery and courage in the face of adversity and inhumanity, and that of his saviours, is truly inspiring.'

OLIVIA MARKS-WOLDMAN,
Holocaust Memorial Day Trust

'This spellbinding book will take you on the streets of 1940s Amsterdam as a Jewish boy twists and turns to remain alive.

'Each page immerses the reader in the sights, sounds and experiences confronting Lex everywhere he looks.

'A captivating account of one boy's survival through his wit, courage and nine lives.'

BARONESS GILLIAN MERRON

Nobody
Lives Here

Nobody Lives Here

A Jewish Childhood in the Occupied Netherlands

LEX LESGEVER

Translated by Babette Lichtenstein
and Jozef van der Voort

Front cover image: Mark Owen/Trevillion Images

Originally published by Boekerij, Amsterdam, The Netherlands, under the title
Nooit verleden tijd, 2010

This English-language edition first published 2023

The History Press
97 St George's Place, Cheltenham,
Gloucestershire, GL50 3QB
www.thehistorypress.co.uk

© Lex Lesgever and Meulenhoff Boekerij bv, Amsterdam, The Netherlands, 2010
Introduction © Babette Lichtenstein, 2023
English-language translation © Babette Lichtenstein and Jozef van der Voort, 2023

British Library Cataloguing in Publication Data.
A catalogue record for this book is available from the British Library.

ISBN 978 1 80399 322 5

Typesetting and origination by The History Press
Printed and bound in Great Britain by TJ Books Limited, Padstow, Cornwall.

Trees for LYfe

I dedicate this book to all the members of my family
who were murdered during this dreadful war

First name	Family name	Birth date	Death date	Place of death
Salomon	Lesgever	26 June 1896	9 July 1943	Sobibor
Grietje	Lesgever-Gompers	24 January 1898	21 May 1943	Sobibor
Wolf	Lesgever	11 August 1920	29 August 1941	Mauthausen
Mozes	Lesgever	6 July 1923	21 May 1943	Sobibor
Marianna	Hakker	16 August 1920	23 September 1942	Auschwitz
Julie	Lesgever-Mug	3 August 1893	1 October 1942	Auschwitz
Wolf	Lesgever	27 August 1917	24 June 1942	Mauthausen
Mietje	Lesgever	23 March 1920	1 October 1942	Auschwitz
Marianna	Lesgever	15 May 1922	30 September 1942	Auschwitz
Saartje	Lesgever	11 October 1890	17 September 1942	Auschwitz
David	Lesgever	9 April 1898	30 September 1943	Blechhammer
Aaltje	Lesgever-Zwaaf	16 April 1898	8 October 1942	Auschwitz
Abraham	Lesgever	14 November 1928	8 October 1942	Auschwitz
Marianna	Lesgever	28 July 1933	8 October 1942	Auschwitz
Jacob	Lesgever	12 April 1900	31 March 1943	Seibersdorf
Saartje	Lesgever-Groen	22 July 1910	10 September 1942	Auschwitz
Marianna-Frederika	Lesgever	10 February 1941	10 September 1942	Auschwitz
Maurits	Lesgever	20 March 1903	21 May 1943	Sobibor
Saartje	Lesgever-Reens	27 April 1902	21 May 1943	Sobibor
Levie	Lesgever	8 February 1938	21 May 1943	Sobibor
Hartog	Lesgever	8 January 1902	21 May 1943	Sobibor
Willem	Verduin	5 March 1924	30 September 1942	Auschwitz
Leentje	Gompers-Rijnveld	6 September 1867	5 February 1943	Auschwitz

First name	Family name	Birth date	Death date	Place of death
Isaac	Gompers	5 January 1895	4 June 1943	Sobibor
Rachel	Gompers-de Jong	3 July 1897	4 June 1943	Sobibor
Simon	Gompers	13 August 1925	30 September 1942	Auschwitz
Mozes	Gompers	5 March 1930	4 June 1943	Sobibor
Herman	Gompers	10 January 1933	4 June 1943	Sobibor
Benjamin	Gompers	29 March 1902	4 June 1943	Sobibor
Esther	Gompers-Beesemer	1 July 1897	4 June 1943	Sobibor
Mina	Gompers	5 July 1935	4 June 1943	Sobibor
Moordes	de Vries	3 October 1891	25 January 1943	Birkenau
Elisabeth	de Vries-Gompers	1 June 1891	9 July 1943	Sobibor
Emanuel	de Vries	5 November 1922	2 July 1943	Sobibor
Robert	Depken	16 November 1886	9 July 1943	Sobibor
Hendrina	Depken-Gompers	10 January 1894	9 July 1943	Sobibor
Albert-Mozes	Depken	5 February 1916	28 February 1945	Central Europe, precise location unknown
Leentje	Depken-Goudsmit	7 January 1920	11 June 1943	Sobibor
Hendrina	Depken	16 September 1941	11 June 1943	Sobibor
Elisabeth	Plukker-Depken	9 May 1917	30 November 1943	Auschwitz
Aron	Zeehandelaar	19 May 1911	31 January 1943	Auschwitz
Leentje	Zeehandelaar-Depken	27 September 1914	14 May 1943	Sobibor

Introduction

This memoir is a gripping and unusual account of a survivor of the Shoah in Holland. With impressively clear recall of his childhood and early teens – he was 11 at the outbreak of the war – Lex Lesgever writes of his years on the run and in hiding in Amsterdam and beyond. It is unusual because Lex was never deported to a death camp, but managed to escape when his family was taken, and then spent about two months on his own, mostly in Amsterdam, sleeping rough in shelters and stairwells, stealing food, trying to keep clean and, occasionally, receiving help from adults. He is caught in the middle of Nazi raids more than once – is hunted, shot at and interrogated at Nazi headquarters – and he grows ever more alert and resilient without losing his sensitivity and humanity. His many lucky and instinctively brilliant escapes are quite breathtaking, and are beautifully described through the eyes of a resourceful but very frightened child. Painting a picture of the unfolding events in Amsterdam during Anne Frank's time in hiding, Lex's memoir complements the reading of her diary.

Before recounting his time as a fugitive, Lex Lesgever describes what life in Jewish Amsterdam was like before the war, focusing on the long-established, close-knit, mostly working-class, loosely religious and vibrant life of Amsterdam's Jewish quarter around the area of Waterlooplein, in which his large family comfortably took part: the Jewish festivals in the streets, the market stalls, the mutual support, the easy living alongside the rest of Amsterdam's population. This gives a historically interesting prelude and highlights the horrific contrast with the devastating events that entirely destroyed this old way of life within such a short time.

Today's visitors to Amsterdam are surrounded by greenery. There are trees along the canals, lavishly planted flowerbeds, wild grasses and weeds growing undisturbed between tram rails, and the inhabitants have been permitted to lift paving stones abutting their houses where flowering climbers are now growing around their front doors and up the brick walls.

It wasn't always so. For about thirty years after the Second World War, Amsterdam was a relatively bare place. The dire need for food and fuel, especially during the Hunger Winter of 1945, had caused many of Amsterdam's trees and even floorboards to go up in flames.

Amsterdam seemed bare in the 1950s and 1960s, but there was something else as well. People walked with their heads lowered, not looking each other in the eye. Evasion was in the air; people were wary of each other. Bullying was rife. Teachers bullied pupils, children bullied younger or weaker ones, anyone in authority bullied citizens, neighbours bullied each other. I lived there and witnessed it.

Growing up in Amsterdam shortly after the Second World War was an unsettling experience for me and my sister. My father, a Jewish musician, had left Germany for

Holland in the early 1930s and had gone into hiding in 1942, at different addresses in and around Haarlem. Immediately after the war he married, and my parents spent a short period in Jerusalem before returning to Holland. They settled in the 'old south' of Amsterdam. We lived in an apartment on Merwedeplein, a few doors away from where Anne Frank and her family had lived before they went into hiding, also in 1942. It had been quite a Jewish neighbourhood, mainly middle class, unlike the old working-class community around Waterlooplein which Lex describes so vividly.

In the 1950s my mother told us about the war years, mainly through anecdotes, and we heard about the Shoah and about the terrible danger my father had been in, as well as the people who had saved him. But outside the walls of our apartment there was a culture of silence. The word 'Jew' was avoided: it was painful to say it or hear it. After reading Lex's sober, poignant and clear descriptions of what happened to him in the streets around Anne Frank's hiding place (and that of many others), I realised that after the war Amsterdam was a city in trauma and denial.

According to my father there had been no antisemitism in the Netherlands before the war. I didn't believe him at the time, but from Lex's anecdotes of his neighbourhood before the occupation I concluded that maybe my father had a point. I began to understand that where fear and terror reign on such scale and intensity for even just five years, many people begin to absorb the prevailing mentality in an attempt to cope with life.

Visitors to Amsterdam today will find the silence around its Second World War history has been broken. Studio

Libeskind's impressive Holocaust Memorial, built close to Lex's old neighbourhood, shows thousands of names of the Amsterdam citizens murdered in the Shoah. Amongst them are the names of all Lex's family members. The shapes of the walls of the open memorial – because of its size only clearly perceived from the air – form the three letters of the Hebrew word 'Remember'.

Lex describes a time when all moral sense had been turned upside down; what was good or bad had lost all meaning. Grown-up men would go hunting for a single child of 13, as happened to Lex, and for much younger children too. People would be turned out of their homes and carted off. In Amsterdam, the Shoah played out with particular viciousness: the German occupation had been headed not by a military commander but by the notorious Nazi A. Seyss-Inquart, who was later tried at Nuremberg and executed. Under his cruel and ruthless rule less than 25 per cent of Dutch Jews survived the Shoah.

It struck me that Lex doesn't name the Shoah explicitly, not with any word. The Hebrew word Shoah means 'calamity', which in its neutrality is a more acceptable word than Holocaust, with its ancient biblical roots in a 'complete burnt offering' on an altar. Maybe the best word for the unimaginable crime is 'Churban', used by Tony Bayfield as the title of his textbook for Holocaust education. It means 'Destruction', and is most often used in connection with the two destructions of Jerusalem and its Temple in 587 BCE and 70 CE.

Growing up under the cloud of this twentieth-century 'Churban' has coloured my outlook on life. I am of course not alone in this. Trying to overcome my fear of it, trying to understand it, come to terms with it, think beyond it, is a constant burden. I therefore had mixed feelings when Jozef van der Voort suggested we translate Lex's memoir together. But I am grateful to him for choosing it and glad to have accepted the challenge. It is a gripping and vivid account of events we should know about and never forget. The boy who emerges from the pages is talking to us all and should become a friend to children of his age, someone they can identify with, as much as they can with Anne Frank.

Another issue which is still hotly debated, and about which Lex tells us in all his innocence of that time, is the involvement of the Joodsche Raad or 'Jewish Council', the body set up by the Nazis as a go-between to reassure Jewish citizens, alleviate their stress and panic, and so aid the smooth organisation of the persecution. When Lex is awaiting deportation with his mother and elder brother Max, and many others, in the Hollandsche Schouwburg, it is likely the Joodsche Raad that secures permission for the smaller children to be escorted across the road to the Jewish Orphanage where there are mattresses to sleep on. And, astonishingly in the circumstances, they are also taken for a walk to the home of someone probably linked to the 'Raad', where they are given hot chocolate. This outing then provides Lex with the opportunity for his first heart-stopping escape.

After his astonishing survival amid the terrible dangers of Amsterdam's streets, Lex is rescued by members of the Dutch resistance and taken to a small agricultural community, Roelofarendsveen, where he spends the rest of the war on a farm working extremely hard and living as a member of the farmer's family. The manner in which the whole village knows and accepts the many Jews hiding amongst them provides a thought-provoking contrast to Lex's experiences in Amsterdam, and opens the reader's eyes to the complicated picture of the infamous German occupation of the Netherlands.

Finally, the memoir is also a 'coming of age' story. Already while working on the farm in Roelofarendsveen, when the farmer is incapacitated by illness for some months, Lex, aged just 16, has to take over, work twice as hard and make business decisions. And when the war ends, he must cope with the terrible fact that not one member of his immediate or wider family has survived the death camps. He returns to the chaos of post-war Amsterdam, where he tries to rebuild his life with scant help from the authorities. After battling with illness (several bouts of tuberculosis), he recovers his health, sets up a successful business and starts a family. The last chapter in the book describes Lex's emotional visit to a concentration camp and is a well-crafted coda to the story.

Lex Lesgever died on 31 December 2019 at the age of 90. Not until he retired did he write down his experiences during the Second World War. After the memoir was published in the Netherlands he gave interviews on radio and talked in schools about his life. Shortly before his death Lex was filmed at home giving testimony for the new National Holocaust Museum in Amsterdam to be opened in 2024. Holocaust education was close to his heart. I admire Lex's dedication to teaching the devastating consequences of a regime's complete loss of moral compass and share his hope that we will 'never forget'.

Babette Lichtenstein
February 2023

Foreword

Although I was born in Amsterdam, I have lived near Leiden for about forty years now. At least three times a week I pass Roelofarendsveen, where I spent a few years during the war. A very special place for me, with very special people.

It's strange really that a village which sheltered such a huge number of fugitives during the war, and thereby helped so many people, has never been given a statue. Few people remember what took place there during the war years, though sometimes I visit Roelofarendsveen to go fishing, and when I happen to bump into an old acquaintance, we may talk about it. Once I called the secretary of the local authority in Roelofarendsveen in search of information, but the good man knew nothing and there was no archive of those days either.

Yet the village and its inhabitants still have a place in my heart of hearts. As far as I'm concerned, many of the people there were made by God Himself. I met them, I got to know them, and I came to love them. I survived the war in part because of them. They warmly welcomed me into their midst, kept me safe and watched over me. But sadly, not even they could do anything for the loss I suffered.

Lex Lesgever
2009

1

There were about twenty centimetres of snow on the ground and an icy easterly wind was blowing. It was an old-fashioned Dutch winter's day in January 1937 and we were on the way back from the funeral of my grandfather, Moos Gompers. It was my first time at a funeral. I was 8 years old. Grandpa Moos was my mother's father. I can still picture him clearly – a real grandpa. A stately, grey-haired old gentleman with aristocratic looks. I know that he made a living in many different ways, but my memory only goes back to his last business, a confectionery wholesaler on Zandstraat in Amsterdam.

Everyone was closely involved in the funeral, as is the Jewish tradition. The coffin was carried to the grave by the immediate family, and then the prayers were recited. Four family members held the ropes and lowered the coffin into the grave. Each of the men in attendance tipped three shovelfuls of sand on top, with close relatives going first. Then it was the turn of friends, followed by the rest of the men, until the grave was full.

I can still hear the dull sound of the sand falling on the wooden coffin; it was a very memorable experience. The occasion was also a very serious one for me, as one's first time at such an event is of course particularly interesting.

The second funeral I attended was that of my little cousin Max. He was the son of my mother's brother Bernhard and he was 6 years old when he died. A few months earlier he had survived the bombing of Rotterdam with his parents and sister. The only thing I knew of his illness was that he had a very swollen tummy. The rest of his body was frail and almost translucent. It wasn't clear then what his illness was, but knowing what we know now, he must have had leukaemia. He died in the winter of 1940. I can vividly recall that funeral too; just about the whole school was there, although he'd only attended for a very short time.

It wasn't until later that I realised I had a relatively large family; I had seventeen uncles and aunts who all had children of their own too. At home there were five of us: my father, my mother, my two elder brothers Wolf and

Lex's mother and father. (Courtesy of Fiety Lesgever)

Max, and myself of course. There were three years between each of us boys.

I was only able to bury two members of that large family. The rest were all murdered in Nazi camps.

My eldest brother was named after Grandpa Wolf, my father's father, and wasn't unlike him in character either. Grandpa Wolf never said much – or rather, he said very little – but what he did say was often to the point. On the way home from school we would walk past grandpa's house and we'd always pop in, because we always felt peckish just after school. Grandpa knew that, and so he always had something tasty for us. Only in hindsight do I realise that he never really gave us sweets; he usually gave us a slice of ginger cake spread so thick with butter that you could leave neat little toothmarks in it. 'That'll oil your gut,' grandpa would say. Then he'd send us home and we'd have to hurry because otherwise mother would get worried. He would plant a kiss on your cheek a bit too hard – I think on purpose – so that the little moustache adorning his upper lip would sting your skin and you'd yell with pain and have to squirm free. If you made enough fuss you'd get a cent by way of consolation.

Grandpa and Grandma Gompers, my mother's parents, lived on Koningsstraat above Veldman's the butcher. If I close my eyes I can still smell the aroma of their kitchen. It was a small kitchen with a window over the counter, which had two Haller kerosene stoves on it. It was a custom in our family that on Friday night one or two grandchildren would have dinner with Grandpa and Grandma Gompers, and I always went over with my brother Max.

After Grandpa Moos died, grandma came to live with us. Grandma had diabetes and was nearly blind. We lived in a fairly big house on Jodenbreestraat. She had grey hair and was a quiet, sweet woman. When you sat with her she would always put her hand on your head without saying anything. Apart from in the evening, that is, when I had to go to bed. I would stand next to her chair in my pyjamas and she'd put her hand on my head, right where my kippah would have been, and say: 'Now *nachtlajene*, pee and off to bed.'

★   ★   ★

I can talk for hours about my grandparents; for the short time that I knew them they were very important to me. I can still hear grandma telling us to say our prayers, wash, brush our teeth and put on our pyjamas. It's awful that so many Jewish people my age have no idea what it is to have grandparents as they all perished in the war; they're missing out on so much without really being aware of it.

All in all I am lucky that I do remember my grandmas and grandpas and all my uncles, aunts and cousins, and when I blow the shofar on Yom Kippur, the Day of Atonement, I stand alone on the bimah and look at the Torah scrolls in the Aron Hakodesh – the Holy Ark – and they are in my thoughts, every last one of them.

★   ★   ★

After we got back from grandpa's funeral and everyone was having coffee, Aunt Cis decided she'd come over to ours for dinner. Aunt Cis was one of my father's sisters and the

Lex, about 3 years old, with a toy car. (Courtesy of Fiety Lesgever)

only one in our family, on father's as well as on mother's side, who wasn't married. She was what we now call emancipated, and for the time she was a little bit special. Aunt Cis had a boyfriend abroad whom we called Uncle Kees. We children liked going to see her, but whenever he was there we weren't welcome.

Aunt Cis coming with us meant that as soon as we got home a civil war would break out between brother and sister. They adored each other as long as they didn't discuss politics because then they'd instantly become virtual enemies. The living room transformed into a kind of parliament with two factions: a socialist party led by my father and a liberal party chaired by my aunt. The discussions would already start at the door and the debate would gradually grow more heated; the volume crept up, but oddly enough the boiling point was always reached during the soup course. Fists would often bang the table so hard that our spoons would jingle on our plates and spatters of soup would land all over the cloth.

All I can recall from these discussions are the names that kept coming up, often including that of Adolf Hitler. At our long table in the dining room we predicted the Second World War. In fact, I'd have to say my family already fought it there, though in their own way, not in the way of Hitler and *Mein Kampf*. At this point my mother would throw herself into the fray. She had spent a year living in Hamburg with her parents as a young girl, but one year had been enough because my grandfather soon saw what was coming. In all those political arguments it was mostly my mother who turned out to be right. Hitler really did come. And he kept his word and did to us what he'd promised in *Mein Kampf*.

We were not exactly an orthodox family, but the traditions were very much present. My brothers and I went to a state school, but on Wednesday afternoons and Sunday mornings we had to go to the Jewish school. I'm not sure if that was to teach us to feel Jewish or to keep us safely off the streets. They absolutely succeeded in teaching us to feel Jewish, but that was inevitable given that we lived on Jodenbreestraat, the heart of Jewish Amsterdam. Jewish New Year was an obvious example of that. Every Rosh Hashanah I remember the street scenes from back then. Those were wonderful days. The most beautiful cards, covered in glitter, would be

Jodenbreestraat, Lex's parental home. (Courtesy of Fiety Lesgever)

pegged on washing lines above the stalls on the street right outside our door, and everyone would wish each other 'Shana Tova' ('Happy New Year').

And all the women shelling nuts in the street. It cost them a lot of effort to strip off the thick green skin and they were left with terribly dirty black hands that they could hardly get clean again.

And then Pesach – Passover – the festival to relive the exodus from Egypt and the escape from slavery. I thought that was one of the most thrilling and beautiful stories from the Old Testament. I recall that on Seder night, which heralded the start of the week of celebration, my grandfather would always make a mistake somewhere in the story. He did it on purpose to see who would correct him; he loved that. The day before Pesach we always went with

Burning of the chometz. (Jewish Museum, Amsterdam)

father to Jonas Daniël Meijerplein – a square named after the first Jewish lawyer in the Netherlands – where people would be standing around empty oil drums in which they lit fires to burn people's chometz for five cents, because during Pesach not a crumb of bread must be left in the house. Then we'd eat nothing but matzos with brown sugar for a whole week.

I loved it on Jonas Daniël Meijerplein – hearing who could yell, 'Chomeeeeetz, chometz, who's still got some chometz?' the loudest and then throwing the scrap of bread you'd brought from home into the fire.

In those days you celebrated part of the festival on the streets – that's how it was. It wasn't just the orthodox Jews who loved those days, but the liberal too. Matzos, horseradish and matzo balls – nothing special really, but the festive spirit was everywhere. Of course, there was something of the ghetto about it, but that was part of the neighbourhood – the resemblance and the pleasant companionship that the people found in each other. Nobody worked during Pesach; everyone was free and out on the streets. That meant a lot of people bumped into each other and wished each other 'Chag Sameach' ('Happy Passover').

We still celebrate Pesach and Rosh Hashanah, but that neighbourhood is gone. Now we just send each other cards or emails, or take out an advert. The rest is only a memory.

★ ★ ★

One thing I remember very clearly about home is the way we were brought up, which was clearly focused on our independence. On Friday afternoons, for example, they would give

*me a certain amount of money and then I'd have to do all
the shopping for Shabbat. No list or anything. If I asked my
mother what to get, she would answer, 'You know what you
always eat on Friday night, so just make sure we have it in
the house.' That meant I had to get fruit from Mr Gokkes
and gherkins from Sarah Scheefsnoet on the Vissteeg, and
then go to another shop to buy Valencia peanuts. And I definitely couldn't get any other peanuts; only Valencia peanuts
would do.*

★ ★ ★

Something else I also recall well is how both my brothers were financially independent from my parents at a
young age. When my brother Wolf left school he was
offered an apprenticeship as a furrier at Maison Modern
on Kalverstraat. He got it through our downstairs neighbour; Mr Leeuwin, the owner of the fur company, was
his brother-in-law. My brother Max was a born dealer,
so he went to work at a wholesale textile business on Sint
Antoniesbreestraat. Max always knew how to find lucrative
things to trade outside his work. You noticed it particularly
on Sinterklaas, or St Nicholas Day, on 5 December – a trad-
itional Dutch family celebration. At our house, Sinterklaas
was a real occasion. I'll never forget the time Wolf took me
to Van Emden, a well-known toyshop on Kalverstraat, and
bought me an electric train. I was standing right next to
him, but I didn't suspect a thing. And then on Sinterklaas
he gave it to me and I still had no idea that it was the exact
same train I'd more or less picked myself! That was the best
part of it for Wolf.

Max, with trumpet. (Courtesy of Fiety Lesgever)

All those happy memories of home are probably what gave me the courage and tenacity to get through difficult times for the rest of my life.

During my boyhood, my only experience of the serious side of life was on schooldays: Monday to Friday from nine to twelve o'clock and two until four. Other than that I remember it as a carefree time – but that soon ended after the war broke out. On the streets the situation wasn't so bad, but at home it was all too clear that anxiety had the upper hand. War was something I think every boy dreamed of in those days. There was something magical and thrilling about it, but you didn't really understand it. At school you learned about the Eighty Years' War; the people had survived that, so surely this wouldn't be so bad either. My father was an eternal optimist, but sadly not a realist. All the roaring and ranting in German on the radio was very ominous and the whole family would listen to it intently. I didn't understand a word myself, but it did make me afraid. You could tell how nervous everyone was after these broadcasts. Words like 'Hitler', '*Mein Kampf*' and 'concentration camps' became commonplace frighteningly quickly.

The arguments between my parents grew fiercer. My mother, who knew what she was talking about, didn't agree with my father at all – that was quite obvious. My mother took Hitler's speeches very seriously while my father would laugh about them and then list all the marvellous technologies which Britain, America and let's not forget Holland could and would use against the German army. Surely it was impossible for a country like Germany to fight on so many fronts at the same time, let alone win. No, it would never come to that. It was just like my father to say such things. He didn't believe there would be a war between Holland and Germany; it was unthinkable. He had no respect at all for the prime minister at the time, who told the people they could sleep soundly in their beds, but as far as war was concerned he agreed with the prime minister that there wouldn't be a long one – end of discussion.

Wolf was of a different opinion, but he never said so. He had a cupboard in his room which was always locked. That was nothing new because he kept his private things in there. Wolf came home at quarter past six every evening and he would walk past the living room straight to his bedroom. In about December 1940 we began to notice that he was coming home every evening with a large bag, passing through with a 'Good evening', and then walking straight to his room, only to re-emerge about fifteen minutes later. My parents started to wonder and after a while they asked Wolf to explain himself. As usual he wasn't very talkative and refused to say anything. My parents assumed that he was bringing home spare skins.

★ ★ ★

People in the fur trade worked with animal hides. Each type of coat needed a certain number of hides and the boss knew exactly how many. But a clever furrier sometimes managed to deliver a beautiful coat with a half or even a whole hide left over. That leftover hide was called a spare skin. You were really supposed to give it back to your boss, but it was often regarded as a well-earned perk.

★ ★ ★

Wolf's behaviour increasingly aroused our suspicions, and since this wasn't how we were brought up, the bomb eventually had to explode. At first he still refused to say anything and he definitely wouldn't let anyone look in his cupboard. One evening father and son had a real row for the first time ever. And I mean real.

Wolf was 18 and, as I said earlier, he was very independent. After a heated argument my mother got permission to go to his room and the cupboard in question was opened. I still remember the long silence that followed. Then she said, 'Your father needs to see this.'

The whole cupboard was packed with food: coffee, tea, sugar, flour, rice and packs of tobacco and cigars. My father was the only one of us who smoked and my brother had even thought of that. There was great bewilderment. Even Max was speechless – and believe me, it took a lot to shut him up. Once this first step had been accepted, the real stockpiling fever started. Sometimes I was allowed to come along on hoarding trips, and occasionally my brothers would start arguing in de Gruyter's over who should be served first. That had me in stitches, at a time when there wasn't much to laugh about, but for the shop girl who had to intervene it was horrible. In the end, nobody ever reaped the benefits of our splendid supplies.

2

I turned 11 on 1 May 1940.

On 10 May I stood with my father on the pavement just in front of our house. Directly over our heads, two small aeroplanes were engaged in a dogfight. I thought it looked a bit like a classical ballet, with these two fragile little planes so elegantly circling and shooting at each other. Moments later we saw one of them whirling towards the ground. 'Pity,' said my father. I asked why and he replied, 'That was one of ours.'

Shots were fired, and I saw lots of little white clouds appear in the clear blue sky. My father said those were shells and explained that you had to be careful because bits of them fell down to earth and could land on your head. Even that I found thrilling. When we got back indoors I told my mother what had happened and she started to cry. I was baffled. I didn't understand anything about the war, nor why she was crying. It was rather exciting to see those two planes looping and diving through the air, trying to avoid each other, and there always has to be a winner, I thought. When it was all over I ran up to the roof and started looking for bits of shrapnel, which were much in demand for swapping between me and my friends. After all, the war would only last a few days, and then it would all be over. So I thought.

That is how simply you see things when you are a boy of 11.

There were no more Dutch soldiers on the streets, and the military police – the Marechaussee – were no longer active either. The first German uniforms appeared, and then things moved quickly.

The first thing to change was my own environment. The mood at home and in the street was different, but not yet for us kids. It only shifted for us when members of the Dutch Nazi party started rioting in our street. They tried to harass people and smashed windows left and right. They also daubed antisemitic slogans on Jewish shops and houses.

One day my teacher announced that a number of children had to move to another school (I attended a state school)

Shop daubed with antisemitic slogans. (Beeldbank WO2/NIOD)

and I told him I didn't want to. The teacher explained that the Germans wanted it. The war was starting to become more and more real to me.

Of course, we didn't really notice that only Jewish children were made to leave the school. After all, being Jewish had never mattered before. Quite often you would be in a street fight and a friend would say, 'If you mess with that Jew then you're messing with me too.' Then you'd know that was a real friend and you'd feel happy and super-strong. Wasn't that what friends were for? But now the word 'Jew' began to take on a different meaning. You saw it more and more in the daily and weekly newspapers, and every Sunday afternoon at Van Tol's cabaret they would proclaim how bad Jews were and that Holland was their victim too. So in my childish eyes the thrill went out of the war and things were very clearly starting to get serious. We stopped collecting and trading shrapnel, as it just reminded us of the reality of the war.

In the meantime we were moved to a different school – one meant only for Jews, of course, so the teachers were Jewish too. You also noticed a change in what you were learning. The lessons didn't appear to be taken so seriously any more; we were allowed to do many more fun things. I was well aware that people seemed to understand that the need for learning was no longer so urgent, and that right now quality of life mattered much more. After all, there was no knowing what other bad things were still in store for us.

It wouldn't be long before we found out.

That came partly through what went on at home. The discussions that you overheard but didn't understand became ever more insistent, and were increasingly held in a whisper to keep you out of the war somewhat and to hold fear at arm's length. The opposite was often the case, of course. The tensions you felt around you every day gave you a vague sense of undefined threat.

Months went by like this, and not a day passed without something happening that occupied our minds. Change had crept into our life at home. Everyone was focused on 'tomorrow'. My grandmother no longer lived with us; she had moved out to stay with an aunt. I didn't know why, but I knew that my parents, and especially my father, didn't agree with it at all. I didn't understand until later that my father was very fond of my grandmother. I even seem to remember that harsh words had been traded with the aunt and uncle who thought it would be better if grandma went to live with them. As a child, the essence of these things escapes you, but your intuition keeps working like a radar and it becomes second nature.

Saturday 22 February 1941

A Saturday afternoon that started like so many other Saturday afternoons. In those days people worked on Saturdays until one o'clock and Jannie, Wolf's fiancée, went to his workplace to pick him up.

It came like a bolt from the blue, and it is still etched into my memory. The war had only just started for us Jews, but for my brother Wolf it was already over. It was the first raid to be carried out, and Wolf and Jannie were right in the middle of it.

At about noon a lot of open cars with armed soldiers inside (members of the *Grüne Polizei*) drove down our street. There had never been such a big show of force before. A car pulled up at every corner and soldiers stormed out. Everything was cordoned off and not even a mouse could have got in or out. It was a terrifying sight. Soldiers screaming at every man the same question: '*Jude?*' Anyone who answered 'yes' was taken away and herded together on Jonas Daniël Meijerplein. There they were forced to kneel and hold up their hands as if they were dangerous criminals

Raid on Jews, Jonas Daniël Meijerplein. (Beeldbank WO2/NIOD)

– and these were people who had probably never hurt a fly.
Nobody knew what was going to happen.

As suddenly as it had started, it was over.

Immediately rumours started flying around. It was
said that the Germans had taken everyone to the Colonial
Institute (now the Royal Tropical Institute). Or that the
detainees would be taken to a camp in Schoorl. No one
knew anything for certain. There was great dismay, and
not only among Jewish people; even the non-Jews were
bewildered by so great an injustice. Grief and outrage seized
everybody, and the most notable result of it was the big
February Strike.

For me, the excitement of the war had now truly worn
off. Suddenly childhood was left behind and you began to
look at life differently. Even your feelings changed; you
suddenly acquired something of that 'grown-up attitude'.
You had to. There was nothing to do any more either. The
street had ceased to be the domain of children; their place
was taken by soldiers with thumping boots, hard rifle butts
and huge, screaming mouths. From that day in February
the street aroused nothing but fear. At any moment, something could happen like on that Saturday. Fortunately we
celebrated my twelfth birthday as normal, in spite of all the
fear and uncertainty, although there wasn't much money
for presents. Even in those times you still cared about mile-
stones like these.

The next raid took place on 11 June 1941 and after that they
became more and more frequent. The situation became
untenable for many people. It started to sink in with everybody that the great deportation had begun, something that

my mother had long been certain would happen.* Stars on your clothes, a J on your identity card, bans on shopping anywhere other than in Jewish stores. The Jewish Council was founded and Abraham Asscher and David Cohen started to help organise the deportations in a 'good' way. Big money changed hands in exchange for a *Sperr*, a certificate of exemption, and everyone did their utmost to delay their transportation. The battle for survival had begun.

---

* Throughout the memoir, 'deportation' refers to the process of rounding up and detaining Jews in transit camps and other locations in the Netherlands. In many cases their actual removal abroad took place weeks or months after the initial round-up.

3

There were often whispers at home about leaving, but my mother wouldn't hear of it. After all, one of her sons had been taken and she didn't know where he was. Imagine if he suddenly came home and she wasn't there. That was unthinkable.

By this point, Wolf had already been gone for several months and no one knew what the Germans had done with the men in that first raid. There were all sorts of rumours, but it wasn't really clear what exactly had happened. Very sporadically, a family would receive a postcard with a message that the deported person was well, but the stamps on them didn't make things any clearer. My brother Wolf was the focal point of everything. His place at the table was forbidden territory, for example; nobody was allowed to sit there. For my mother, the worst and most unimaginable thing had happened: she had lost a child. The radio had to stay switched off; no more records were played on the gramophone.

My Dutch mother spoke German without an accent; the Germans all thought she was one of them. One day she decided to venture an attempt to find out what had happened to Wolf. She took the train to The Hague and visited the headquarters of Arthur Seyss-Inquart, the

Reichskommissar of the Netherlands. After being made to wait for an hour, she was led into his room – the lion's den. She sat down in front of him and greeted him in German. It must have sounded so authentic to him that he started to make small talk with her. At one point he asked her how long she'd been in Holland and she had to admit that she'd lived here all her life. What was more, she'd been born here. When he asked where she had learned to speak German so well, she told him that she'd lived in Hamburg for a while with her parents, and that she'd gone to school there too. After some more chit-chat he abruptly asked her what it was that she'd come for. She told him that her son had been taken and that she didn't know what had happened to him or where he was living at that time. He asked her for his full name. Once she'd told him, he opened a large drawer which contained an index card box. In two seconds flat, he had Wolf's card on the table, and on seeing his details he flew into a rage and asked my mother: 'Are you a Jew?' He screamed the question, but my mother didn't bat an eyelid.

'Didn't you read the sign? "Forbidden for Jews"?'

My mother conceded that she had seen it. After some more yelling, Seyss-Inquart got himself back under control and even started to answer her question. He said that Wolf was working somewhere in Germany and doing well. They all had to work hard, but they were also being looked after. She absolutely didn't need to worry. She asked him when Wolf would be allowed to come home again, but the Reichskommissar couldn't give her an answer. After that she had to leave his office and he warned her that she mustn't dare to set one foot in the building again. If she ever tried to bother him he would have her thrown in jail.

At the end of June there was suddenly another raid and everyone looked all over the place for shelter. No one dared to stay on the street. It always reminded me of musical chairs: the whistle blew and everyone scattered in all directions.

One man, Joop Stork from Ostadestraat, fled into our house. Strange that I still remember his name and where he lived. This raid took much longer than usual. My father sat talking with the man and it must have been about two o'clock when my father called me over and explained what I had to do: 'Mr Stork here lives on Ostadestraat. Take the tram to his house and tell his wife that he's safe. If need be, he'll stay here the whole night.'

I went up to the attic, made my way via the gutter to the house next door and climbed inside through the attic window. Then I went down the stairs and walked through Mr Borkulo's tobacco shop out onto the street. That wasn't dangerous for me because, with my blond hair and blue eyes, I didn't 'look' Jewish at all, and I never wore a star on missions like these. So I walked to the tram stop without feeling that I was doing anything dangerous. The number nine tram to the Munt went past Waterlooplein, where I saw that the Germans had once again herded together all the Jews they'd got hold of.

It was rather a handy spot for the Germans because there was already a fence. Looking back, I realise now that it didn't shock me any more – you got used to it, in a sense. On reaching Ostadestraat, I rang the bell for an apartment on the second floor. A short woman opened the door and I went upstairs. If I remember rightly, the family had six children. I thought that was rather a lot; it wasn't what I was used to.

I said what I had to say and went to leave, but Mrs Stork gave me a glass of lemonade and a biscuit and started asking me all sorts of questions. For instance, she wanted to know exactly what happened in these raids. I remember thinking it was a very strange question: didn't we all know how it worked? I didn't realise, of course, that these people lived in Amsterdam South, and that the early raids only took place in our 'Jewish quarter'. When I told them what had happened, the two older children looked at me with something like envy, and I suspected that they found it all rather exciting and felt they were missing out. Just as I got up to go home, their father walked through the door. He said that fortunately the raid had finished half an hour after I'd left.

When I got home, no one asked how it had gone, which I found rather strange and I must say it made me a little angry. Only the following afternoon, while he was reading the newspaper, did my father ask, without looking up, 'Were you frightened yesterday?'

The situation for Jews got worse by the day and many people suddenly disappeared because they'd been taken away or had gone into hiding. Still others turned themselves in after receiving a summons, but you never knew for sure. You'd just suddenly realise that someone wasn't around any more, and then you'd assume that they'd handed themselves in, been deported or organised a hiding place. The latter option wasn't for everyone, though, because first of all you had to know where to go, and then you often had to put down an awful lot of cash for it. Not everyone who sheltered people in their home did so from the goodness of their hearts; many of them also did it for the money.

There's no shame in that, of course, but it did happen some-times that, when the money ran out, the people were asked to look for another address.

One Sunday evening in August 1941 my father called for me and asked if I remembered our occasional visits to Mr and Mrs Schepers, who ran a cafe in Hoevelaken. The cafe stood on a fork in the road and that was also its name: De Driesprong.

My father explained that I had to run an errand for him. The next day I was to put on a vest in which my mother had sewn a pouch. My father told me all this in his own calm and quiet manner, and the way he presented it sug-gested there was nothing special going on. He picked up a small box with a sliding lid; I think it had originally held a brand of aspirin, and I even recall the name: Saridon. He slid the lid open and at first all I could see was a bit of cotton wool. When he lifted it up, there was a load of sparkling diamonds. I knew they were diamonds, but otherwise none of it meant much to me. Just as well. I was told that I had to go to the station the next morning, buy a return ticket to Amersfoort and then take a bus from Amersfoort to the cafe in Hoevelaken, where I had to hand over the box and the recipient would put a lot of money in my pouch in return. Once I was back in Amsterdam, I wasn't to bring the money home; instead I had to go straight to Mr Beesemer. Mr Beesemer lived above Keizer, the butcher's shop a few doors down from us.

The next morning I set off. At the station I bought a return to Amersfoort and looked for a window seat. In the seats opposite me were a man and a woman who looked at me with admiration, or maybe surprise. The woman asked me cautiously if I often travelled alone by train and I confirmed this with studied nonchalance. The journey went smoothly and I almost forgot about the little box I was wearing on my chest. With the help of a bus driver in Amersfoort I found the right bus and got on.

When I entered the cafe Mr Schepers came towards me, shook my hand and took me to the kitchen. His wife put her arms around me and gave me a big kiss, and then immediately started making me some fried eggs on bread. It wasn't until I began to eat that I realised I was rather peckish. Once the food was all gone, the cafe owner took me to the bedroom, where I had to take off my shirt. He took the little box and marvelled at the contents. Then he gave me the money, which I tucked away safely inside the secret pocket in my vest, as if this was all completely normal. When we came back downstairs Mrs Schepers had a mug of hot chocolate ready for me. After a little while Mr Schepers said that the bus would arrive any moment now, and after I'd said goodbye to Mrs Schepers, we went outside together, sat down side by side on the kerb and waited for the bus.

Back in Amsterdam, I boarded the number eight tram, which took me home. When I reached Breestraat I did as I'd been told: I went straight to the Beesemer family's apartment block and rang the bell. Once I was upstairs, Mr Beesemer took me into the kitchen and removed the money from my vest. I didn't know what to say. Mr Beesemer just looked at me, touched my cheek lightly and told me I'd best go home quickly. So I said my goodbyes and went home. My mother was waiting for me and took a deep breath when she saw me. A moment later my father came in and simply asked if everything had gone well and if I'd been to see Mr Beesemer. When I said yes he gave me a hug. I didn't understand much of it.

The next morning I happened to look at the Beesemers' house and saw that the curtains were still closed, and that's how they remained from then on. I've never seen any of the family since. Maybe they managed to go into hiding, or maybe they were deported after all – I have no idea. In those days you simply didn't talk about things like that.

4

One day in September I was eating with my father at the kitchen table when he said I had to do something for him again. I felt curious because, whenever my father said that, it was bound to be something really interesting. Over time I had started to like the fact that there were things I could do for him. I rather enjoyed the excitement that came with it, probably because I hadn't grasped the true nature or the seriousness of these adventures. My father took me up to the floor where he kept his canaries and lifted me onto his lap. He only did that when we had to discuss something private. It took him a moment to begin, as if he found it difficult – as if he was worried that he might be asking too much.

'On Friday you must do something very important for me. You know that many people are being taken away. You also know that some people are going into hiding. Well, children don't go into hiding, they just go and "stay with someone" for a long while. That's what we call it. Doortje, your cousin Lea's daughter, has to go and stay with someone too, and I want you to take her there. On Thursday I'll fetch her from Lea's and then she'll spend the night with us. On Friday morning at nine o'clock you'll take her to Amersfoort, and from there by bus to Hoevelaken, where she'll stay for the time being. You just have to make sure that you're the one who answers if anyone asks you anything, and if they do, you tell them, "I'm taking my sister to an aunt who lives in the country; she's going there on holiday for two weeks." And if you behave in the same way as you did the last few times, nobody will suspect a thing. I'll take you both to the train station myself on Friday.'

To me, it was starting to become an exciting story. Sometimes, as a child, you could no longer see the difference between a dangerous situation and a test to see who was the cleverest. I think I needed that feeling, because if I'd realised how dangerous it was, I would never have dared to go through with it.

That Thursday afternoon, a smiling Doortje arrived at our place. She was a little girl of 6 with a head of blonde Shirley Temple ringlets which danced around her pretty face. Everyone talked to her, fussed over her and admired her. We had so much fun that afternoon. Only my mother was quiet and sad, but back then I didn't understand why.

On Friday morning my father, Doortje and I left for the station. I can still see my mother's face as she said goodbye to Doortje. It was a good thing I didn't understand what saying goodbye meant to people at that time. Doortje was walking between me and my father. She was a bouncy little thing. On the way she talked nineteen to the dozen, because as an only child she hadn't often gone to stay with other people, of course, and she thought it was great fun. My father, who was really very tall, was literally looking down on us, and I wonder now what he must have felt. In any case, he must have been convinced that our journey was completely safe, as he would never have let it happen otherwise. He also must have had an unshakeable trust in me. The fact that we didn't look at all Jewish was naturally to our great advantage.

When we arrived at Muiderpoort station, my father said goodbye to us both. I could sense that it was a difficult moment for him. He lifted Doortje up and kissed her a few times. Then he put her back down and gave me a penetrating look. He put his hand on my head and said, 'I'll see you tonight. Make sure you don't get in late, as you know your mother gets very worried.'

Doortje skipped alongside me as we went into the station hall, and wanted to know exactly what I was doing. She had to know how and why I was buying the tickets, what the lady behind the counter asked me, and why she only talked to me and not her. While I was asking the guard what platform our train would be departing from, a woman tried to interfere. I probably gave her such a scathing look that she immediately turned around and resumed her own journey.

The train ride went smoothly. Doortje knelt on her seat and looked through the window. My mother had given us a few buttered slices of homemade cake in case we were hungry on the way, but those obviously vanished before we had even left the station. Doortje chattered non-stop, as if she went on trips like this every day. She didn't ask why I was the one going with her and not Uncle Bull (that's what people called my father because he was such a strapping man). She didn't mention her own parents, and it all seemed so normal that none of the other travellers paid us any attention. By now, of course, I had a growing awareness that we were doing things that weren't completely risk-free. But I never had any thoughts or feelings of fear. My father never said the word 'dangerous' either. He had me do things that were evidently very normal for me at that time. Later, and not even all that much later, this bit of training would often save my life. In any case, every day you survived was a victory, though you never stopped to dwell on it.

It must have been about half past eleven when we arrived in Hoevelaken. Mrs Schepers picked Doortje up, sat her on the billiard table and gave her a big kiss. It was as if she'd come back home after a long absence, and yet they'd never met before. A little later we were sitting around the table for lunch. I recall that Doortje immediately felt comfortable there. She skipped around as if she were at home – even I was struck by that. I can still remember how they put the used tea leaves out to dry on a wooden tray behind the house so they could use them again. There was a war on, after all, and goods like these were already getting scarce. It's bizarre how you remember things like that. Doortje seemed to have no problems at all. She happily ate and chattered away. She didn't say a word about her parents or anything that would remind her of home. Later we went to play for a bit in the garden, because I was also still a child, after all. Eventually Mrs Schepers called me to say that someone would take me to the station because otherwise I'd get home too late, and the last I saw of Doortje was her hanging upside down from the rings and looking at me between her legs, laughing as she said goodbye. She was probably moved on from Hoevelaken and placed with other people.

★ ★ ★

After the war, when we wondered what might have happened to her, the answer was a long time coming. We heard by chance that she was still alive, but no one wanted to give us her address – that was up to Doortje. By all accounts, she'd got married. When she was informed that she still had a living relative who would love to meet her, she let us know that she didn't want to be in touch with anyone from her past.

★ ★ ★

The raids came more and more frequently, and they weren't restricted to our neighbourhood any more either. The Germans made many Jews move from other parts of Amsterdam into the Jewish quarter, but they often didn't even bother with that and deported Jews without any stop on the way.

One day in February 1942, my mother put a small pan in my hands and informed me that I had to take it to Nanny Blog.

Nanny Blog lived across the way from us at number 64, on the first floor. Everyone over the age of 50 in our neighbourhood was automatically called 'Nanny', and Mrs Blog was no exception. Nanny Blog had gone blind from diabetes, just like my grandma, but the community looked after her. The baker, the greengrocer and the butcher delivered to her door, and her neighbours fetched everything else from the shops.

I crossed the street to deliver my little pan of soup, as usual. She would pour the soup straight into another pan, wash our pan and then hand it back to me. While Nanny was busy doing that, I looked through the window and

Amsterdam Jews prepared for deportation. (Beeldbank WO2/
NIOD/H. Heukels)

saw three groups of soldiers coming down the street. By
the time I turned round, the bell was already ringing. I
flew into the corridor and stormed upstairs. Nanny Blog
opened the door and the soldiers marched into the apartment. Nanny had to put on her coat and go with them
straight away. I sat hidden in a nook in the stairwell and
made myself as small as I could. They evidently had very
precise orders because the rest of the house was left undisturbed. From where I was sitting dead quiet in my corner,
I could hear exactly what happened directly below me.
Nanny Blog would have been about 65, and when they
were halfway down the stairs, she asked one of the soldiers
if he would help her as she could barely see any more. The
man replied, 'Of course', and then he must have given her

a push, because I heard her fall head over heels down the stairs and scream with pain.

The whole time my mother had stood by the window looking for me. When she saw the Germans going upstairs at Nanny Blog's, she wanted to go straight out to fetch me. My father had to hold her back with all his might and reassure her that I would know how to save myself. He was proven right in the end, but that afternoon seriously traumatised me. I don't know how long I stayed sitting in that nook, and for the life of me I can't remember going back home.

Suddenly everything was moving at lightning speed. Every day the green lorries did their rounds and people were taken to the police station on Waterlooplein, from where they were deported. Every day I saw so many people leave, laden with backpacks and winter coats even though it was high summer.

At home we kept the shutters down day and night and stuck a piece of paper to them with the words 'To let'. That way the building looked empty, and when the *Grüne Polizei* went past they would say: '*Hier wohnt keiner*' ('Nobody lives here'). Then we'd hear the tramp of those lousy boots slowly fade away. In this way, we spent about three months in hiding inside our own house. I did the shopping. I got out onto the street by climbing along the roof gutter and then heading down through the tobacco shop next door. Mr Borkulo always winked at me as I left his shop. Then I'd find myself standing outside our own front door, and I would look up furtively. I no longer went shopping in our own neighbourhood. My family never went outside any more, so it would have looked very strange to everyone if I suddenly walked into a shop. I wasn't allowed to visit the same store twice in a row either. I always had to make sure of the most important thing: that nobody ever noticed me.

During the next of the countless raids, I was away from home. I can't remember where I'd gone; I even think I might have been away for two nights. When I came back in through the skylight, my mother was waiting for me, and as soon as I'd hopped down from the windowsill, she grabbed me and stared into my eyes. I still remember that I saw something in her face – something I'd never seen before. Then she said, 'We should celebrate.' I looked at her, uncomprehending, but she kept staring at me and I started laughing nervously.

'Did you know,' she asked, 'that it was your birthday yesterday? You're 13 now.'

'No,' I replied, and then it sunk in that my birthday had simply passed me by unnoticed. I'd forgotten my own birthday – but I think it was worse for my parents than for me.

My mother gave me six guilders. I thought it was an amazing present: I'd never had so much money before. Fortunately for my mother, I was so pleased with those six shining coins that it must have softened the pain somewhat. Later I realised what strange times we were living in. When you think about it, it's unimaginable that a child would let their birthday pass by unnoticed. After all, you normally count the nights.

From that June, in 1942, the most terrible things started to happen more and more often.

Many people were already gone, and so the net was drawn ever tighter around those Jews that remained. Uncle Bernhard, the father of little Max, was living with his wife Esther on Koningsstraat, above my grandparents' apartment. My mother sent me there regularly to bring them food because they hardly went out any more either. I also went to see them whenever Mr and Mrs Schepers from De Driesprong brought goods from the black market, because some of them were for Aunt Esther. One day I was supposed to take some things to Uncle Bernhard and Aunt Esther at five o'clock. I asked my mother if I could spend the night with them, and she said yes. I liked going there; I could at least walk up and down the stairs as normal, and there wasn't as much sneaking around. I was also happy there because it was the same building that I used to love visiting when Grandpa and Grandma Gompers still lived there.

Aunt Esther and Uncle Bernhard had a little daughter, Marianne. She was just about the only child I was still allowed to spend any time with. Playing in the street with other children was off the cards. Marianne was a few years younger than I was, but that wasn't a problem for me. However much I was getting used to being around grown-ups, I had to think like a grown-up too, and that wasn't always very nice. You had to be on your toes far too much; you had to deal with things that no child should really have to deal with.

Marianne and I didn't have to go to bed early because we didn't go to school any more, but at nine o'clock it was bedtime nonetheless.

5

That night I was woken by my mother bending over me, her face anxious. There was someone else behind her. A man. His face seemed familiar to me, but when you're woken up in the middle of the night you don't come to your senses straight away.

My mother kissed me and told me to get dressed. She went downstairs and I heard her talking with Aunt Esther and Uncle Bernhard. Then the man who looked so familiar came in and smiled at me, and I suddenly remembered: it was Mr Kroon, a policeman from the station on Jonas Daniël Meijerplein. He was a nice man with a friendly face. He always gave you your ball back when you kicked it over the low wall of the police station. He would come down the steps pretending to look angry, hand you the ball and tell you and your friends to beat it.

When I asked him what time it was he replied that it was midnight. Then the truth sank in: we'd been caught. It was our turn now. That was a possibility I'd never considered before. The freedom I'd enjoyed all those months never let me feel that we were in any real danger because my parents stayed safely at home and I did the shopping, as no one ever took any notice of me. Amid all the misery, I lived a tense but carefree existence. It had never occurred to me that there would ever come a day when we wouldn't be able to avoid our fate any longer.

By now Marianne had woken up. She sleepily asked me what I was doing, and I replied that I was getting dressed because I had to leave. Immediately she asked if she could come with me, and I said no. When she asked where I was going, I stopped pulling on my socks and at that moment my fear tipped over into panic. I didn't know what to tell her, and when my mother came in she urged me to hurry. Max was already waiting at the police station and she didn't want him to be taken away without us. Once again, Marianne asked where I was going and I told her I had to go with my mother.

I couldn't recall ever having been out on the street in the middle of the night before, and I found it quite eerie. There were Germans everywhere with Jews they had seized, who were carrying rucksacks, suitcases and winter coats. The street itself was pitch black and, although it was summer, I was cold. I was walking between my mother and Mr Kroon. My mother was holding my hand and that made me a little less afraid, but I instinctively took Mr Kroon's hand too. He looked down at me with a friendly smile.

As we were crossing the Sint Antoniesluis bridge, a car belonging to the *Grüne Polizei* pulled up next to us and a German man told us to get in: '*Einsteigen!*'

Mr Kroon talked to the man. Then we were allowed to walk on. We passed our building, with the shutters covering the windows and the 'To let' notice still showing. We turned off Jodenbreestraat on to Lazarussteeg, where the police station was. Then we went up the steps, through the doors and into the entrance lobby, and through the next set of doors I could see my brother Max waiting for us. The place was packed with people. There were rucksacks and thick winter coats everywhere. My mother pointed at one of the rucksacks. 'That's yours,' she said. I didn't know I owned one. She told me what was in it – my clothes, a first aid box. One thing she expressly pointed out was a balaclava with ear flaps, which I had to take great care of. It might well be very cold where we were going and then I would really need that hat. I had heard something about Siberia at some point, but I had no idea where that was and I hadn't a clue what all this might mean. When Max led me over to a tap so I could have a drink, I asked him where father was and he told me what had happened that evening.

At about half past six, they had suddenly heard the front door being kicked in. My father had shouted for everybody to follow him and gone out via the gutter – the same route I had taken so often. He wanted to get to Mr Borkulo's shop. He had opened the window and climbed out with my mother onto the gutter. Max was the only one still inside, and he was meant to shut the window behind him once he had climbed out. But he never got that far. When the Germans stormed into the room and grabbed Max, my mother turned back. She refused to leave him behind on his own and my father had already gone. At the police station she had gone to Mr Kroon because he wasn't one of the *fout* or 'wrong' policemen who collaborated with the Germans. (I should point out here that when a policeman was 'wrong', it didn't always mean that he agreed with what was happening to the Jews – unlike the so-called 'black police'. Those were trained by the Germans in Schalkhaar, and they persecuted the Jews even more fanatically than many of the Germans.)

My mother had asked Mr Kroon if he could arrange for the two of them to go and pick me up from Koningsstraat. She was afraid that if the *Grüne Polizei* went, they might take my uncle and aunt as well. Mr Kroon had tried to persuade her to leave me behind, saying that he would see if he could find a safe place for me somewhere, but she had no intention of leaving me to face my fate alone. She'd rather look after me herself.

In the course of the night we were taken to the Hollandsche Schouwburg, a theatre that was being used as a deportation centre, and once we got there the fear really took hold.

People were walking around with lists and you could hear names being called out constantly. The theatre had changed. The seats were still laid out in neat rows and the stage curtains were open, but the drama was taking place in the auditorium and the audience was standing on the stage: men and women wearing armbands and men in SS uniforms.

There were even a few things for sale, but Max warned me against spending the six guilders from my birthday. He advised me to save them because you never knew how badly you might need them at some point.

Otherwise we all just sat around waiting. The only thing you could do was walk up and down a bit or get some fresh air in the courtyard.

The next afternoon, when the loudspeakers announced that the children should line up in the hall ready to go to the crèche, Max told me to join them. I was really far too old, but I was short, which made me look younger. The crèche was in a building opposite the Hollandsche Schouwburg, and the children being held in the theatre were taken there each night.

When we were ready to leave, our mothers crowded around us to catch a possible last glimpse of their children. Then we crossed over Plantage Middenlaan, flanked by SS men. It wasn't more than forty metres' walk. At the crèche we were taken to a hall with mattresses in rows on the floor. You had to undress and were given a kind of horse blanket. It took a long time before I fell asleep that night. Now and then I heard a child crying. I thought they were homesick. It didn't occur to me that they might be just as frightened as I was.

The list for transportation to Westerbork, the transit camp where Dutch Jews were held prior to deportation, had already been announced but we weren't on it yet. If you

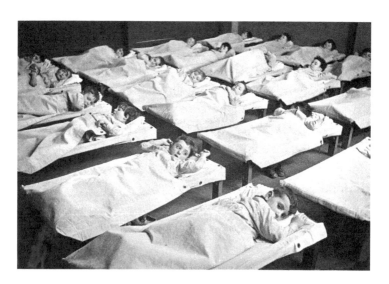

Dormitory in the crèche at Plantage Middenlaan. (Jewish Museum, Amsterdam/Collection Jaap van Velzen)

were very lucky you could wait for as long as a week, but I think that must have involved some favouritism. When we children were brought back to the theatre the following morning to rejoin our families, Max took me aside and told me that small groups of children were sometimes taken for a short walk to 5 Plantage Parklaan.

Max. (Courtesy of Fiety Lesgever)

That was the Leeuwin family's house, our downstairs neighbours who owned the mattress shop on Jodenbreestraat. Max urged me to get into one of those groups; he said that once I got to the Leeuwins' I would have a chance to escape because I knew the exact layout of the house, given that I had been there often enough. I looked at him as if he had gone mad but he just carried on saying things that sounded insane to me – things I didn't want or dare to think about. 'Once you've escaped, get yourself to Hoevelaken as soon as possible, because once you're there everything will be OK. Just tell them what happened here.'

I asked him if he'd gone meshuga – didn't he know how dangerous this was?

He looked me square in the eye. 'Don't you realise that everything you've done these last few months has been dangerous? Trust me, you'll make it.'

I didn't understand a thing. The only feeling I had was a vast emptiness, I couldn't think any more. Then it was all too much for me and I started weeping inconsolably. This was the moment when all the tensions of the last few months came out, and all Max had done was stoke my panic even further.

But Max carried on unsparingly. 'Father has probably gone there too; I expect he's there already.'

That gave me a shock. Where could father be? I had no idea.

That evening we had to go back to the crèche, but when I joined the queue, an SS man suddenly grabbed me and yelled something at me, and then at one of the marshals. I was rigid with fear, although I didn't even know what he had shouted. Fear was the only thing you felt in the face of a screaming German. I was utterly miserable and didn't immediately know what to do. Not that there was anything I could have done – everything moved so fast that you were powerless and at the mercy of other people's actions. Suddenly a man came running towards us. It was Mr Sal Hamburg.

★ ★ ★

For years I attended a school five minutes' walk from home. It was a predominantly Jewish school, of course, as it was in a neighbourhood where lots of Jewish children lived. Both my brothers had also gone there.

At that school I was taught by Mr De Jong, a great teacher who had a Christian background but was nonetheless very much at home with us. It was therefore very hard for him to have to tell us that all Jewish children had to leave and register at a school on Smitstraat, where I stayed for a year. Then it was decided that I would be placed in a school closer to home – the A.B. Davidsschool on Valckenier Street – where my teacher was Mr Hamburg.

★ ★ ★

And now Mr Hamburg was suddenly here. He stood talking for a while with the SS man and then I was put back in the queue.

That night I fell asleep more quickly than the previous one. The next day was the same as the one before, with the difference that at eleven o'clock a small group of children were lined up to be taken for a walk. I remembered what Max had told me about this, but I had immediately pushed all that ridiculous talk to one side. I was with my mother and that was where I belonged. And yet, without much thought, I joined that line of children. Nobody took any notice of me. Strangely enough I didn't feel afraid or nervous; I had slipped back slightly into my former adventurous mode.

When we got outside, we turned right towards the Hortusplantsoen and crossed the road at the corner of Plantage Parklaan. I realised we really were on the way to Mr and Mrs Leeuwin's house. When we walked through the door, Mrs Leeuwin spotted me and immediately came over. To my surprise, Mr Leeuwin remained very grave and didn't show any sign of pleasure at seeing me. I didn't understand it, but I thought that might be the appropriate response to a moment like this.

We were standing in a room which I had visited so often with my parents, under such different circumstances. The children all got something to drink. When my cup was empty, I took it to the kitchen as always, since I knew the way well. I looked through the kitchen window at the garden. Just then I was all alone, and I don't remember what went on inside my head, but with a vacant, blank feeling, I opened the door to the garden and stepped outside. Then everything seemed to speed up. I ran all the way to the bottom of the garden and climbed over the fence into the neighbours' garden. I looked around but there was nobody to be seen. Then I climbed over the next fence and landed in an alleyway that led to Plantage Muidergracht. Once I got there I froze, incapable of moving.

The street was deserted and I had no idea what to do. Luckily I remembered the Jewish star that my mother had sewn on to my coat, on German orders, and in a panic I started to pick at it. When I'd got it off I quickly threw it down a kerbside drain and then frantically looked around, terrified that someone might have seen me. But thank goodness there was still nobody around.

Then reality started to sink in. I was on the street and I was free – but what now? My hand went to my back pocket and with relief I felt my six guilders were still there. I walked towards Roetersstraat. No problems there – though why would there be? I'd been criss-crossing the streets on my own for months already, because who was interested in a little blond boy without a star? Only now that little blond boy felt like the whole world was staring at him. I kept walking without really knowing where I was going. After a while I came to myself again and found I'd made it as far as Weesperzijde. I stopped by the river and gazed for some time at my reflection in the still water. Then I burst into tears. A woman passing by asked me what was the matter. That terrified me even more. What could I say? I randomly blurted the first thing that came into my head: 'My ball fell into the water.'

The woman walked on. It was getting later and later and I still wasn't sure where to go. Then I had an idea: I would go to Haarlemmerstraat to see my 'uncle', Joop Meeuwissen.

Uncle Joop was a friend of my father's. He ran a pet shop and my father always went there to buy his canaries and birdseed. He ought to be able to help me, I thought. When I got there at around five o'clock, Uncle Joop had just gone out, but Lena, the woman who'd kept house for him for many years, took me to the small room behind the shop and asked after my father. I didn't know what to say and started to cry again. She took me onto her lap and tried to comfort me. She washed my face with a wet cloth and just then Uncle Joop came in. He asked what was the matter but I couldn't utter a word. After I'd calmed down a bit and Lena had gone home I told him everything that had happened. He looked at me and for a moment he didn't know what to say either. Then he told me I could stay the night, but because he had a shop that was frequented by friend and foe alike, he thought it was too dangerous to keep me there for long. I said I knew where I could go the next day, but he replied that it was better if I didn't tell him.

So I spent that night at Uncle Joop's. He did his best to be nice to me but I couldn't help feeling utterly miserable. Next morning I woke up early, even though I'd been up late the previous night. I heard Lena come in. By the time

Uncle Joop and I had taken turns washing and getting dressed in the small kitchen, she had made us a sandwich each and was pouring tea. I noticed that she kept giving me sidelong glances. It was obvious that she felt sorry for me, but pity was something I had no use for. I wanted to look tough, so I made her feel that I had no time for her sympathy, but that was just a front because on the inside I was terribly afraid.

I left Uncle Joop's at around noon. After half an hour's walk I found myself on Damrak, where I stopped to consider where I could go. I had no idea. When I started walking again, it struck me that I was close to Nieuwmarkt, which meant I was near my Uncle Bernhard and Aunt Esther's apartment. I wondered if I ought to go there, since that was where I had been taken into custody. They were bound to have noticed my absence at the theatre by now, and they might come looking for me at that address. When I reached the familiar surroundings of their neighbourhood, I walked up and down Koningsstraat a few times hoping to catch a glimpse of my uncle or aunt. They had a small business opposite their house where they made roly-poly toys with the help of two girls, but because of the war the place was closed. I sat down on the doorstep of their shop, waiting to see if anyone would come out, and after five minutes, four members of the *Grüne Polizei* emerged from the alleyway. I froze, as if I were paralysed. I had only one thought: they're looking for me. As if they had nothing better to do. They passed right by but barely noticed me. When they'd gone, I leapt to my feet and got out of there. I didn't dare go up to the apartment. I never saw Uncle Bernhard, Aunt Esther or Marianne again.

Grüne Polizei on Rokin, Amsterdam. (Beeldbank WO2/NIOD/ August Seagers)

Back on Nieuwmarkt, I wandered along the market stalls. There were only a few people around as there wasn't much on sale any more. As I walked past a food stall, I suddenly noticed that I was hungry, but I didn't dare buy anything. I only had guilders, and that wasn't what a child would normally have in his pocket. Besides, if you wanted to buy bread you needed not only money, but also food coupons, and I didn't have any of those. I've often thought back to that bizarre situation: having money, but not being able to buy anything.

A little further along I came to a stall where they sold fizzy drinks and *taaipoppen* – a kind of gingerbread man. The stall-holder was talking to his neighbour. Then I did something I'd never done before: I grabbed a *taaipop* and tucked it under my coat. It happened so quickly that it shocked even me, and the stall-holder didn't notice anything. I strolled away as casually as possible and ate my stolen meal on Geldersekade.

By now it was already five o'clock and I was starting to feel very anxious. I walked back down Koningsstraat but didn't see anyone from my family. I watched the upstairs windows for a time but nothing moved. Panic overtook me again and all I could think to do was to go back to the theatre and hand myself in. But as I went to put my plan into action, I remembered my brother Max. I was meant to go to Hoevelaken. What had stopped me? I'd been too afraid to even think of it. Now it was too late.

It was nearly seven o'clock by now and I was still wandering the streets. The place where I had felt like a fish in water as a child now seemed more like my enemy. Previously I used to roam around outside all the time and routinely came home late. But at least I had a home, no matter how late it was. I wound up on Geldersekade again, and when I looked at the canal I spotted an air raid shelter under the bridge, just above the water. There were steps on each side leading down to it, but nobody used it any more because there were no more air raids.

It was nearly eight o'clock – time for me to be off the streets, as Jews weren't allowed to be outside after eight. It didn't occur to me at all that as far as the outside world was concerned I wasn't a Jew any more, as I had thrown my star down the drain. By doing that, I had become Aryan for the remainder of the war, which meant I could be outside until midnight. I carefully went down into the shelter and sat on one of the wooden benches attached to the walls. I stared blankly into space for a while, not knowing what else to do, but then fatigue got the better of me. I lay down on the bench and soon fell into a deep sleep.

6

I didn't know how long I'd been asleep but when I woke up it was still dark. I lay for a while on the bench and then I heard the church bells of the Zuiderkerk strike five o'clock. That meant I had to wait another hour before I was allowed out; it was the same rule for Jews and gentiles alike. I was stiff and cold, but luckily it was summer, so it could have been worse. When I heard the bells strike six, I went up onto the street. My first destination was the pump at Nieuwmarkt for a drink of water. I tried to wash my face, but with limited success. Passing some shops, I glanced into a window and noticed how dishevelled I looked. I attempted to spruce myself up a bit and smooth down my clothes, but that didn't make much difference either. I was aware that it couldn't be a good thing to look like that and I had the feeling that everybody was staring at me.

At this point my stomach started to rumble too, so when I passed a greengrocer's on Koningsstraat a little later, I quickly snatched an apple. I had clearly lowered my values and standards somewhat. I ran on to Oudeschans and ate my breakfast. Then I went down Batavierstraat and sat on the front step of my old school on Uilenburgerstraat. It had just turned eight o'clock. A quarter of an hour later the first children started to arrive, and as always they played football in front of the entrance. I saw many familiar faces but didn't dare to stay much longer. In any case, I didn't belong there any more. I went back to Koningsstraat, hoping that this time I would catch a glimpse of my uncle and aunt. I gathered my courage and rang the bell, but no one opened the door. On my second attempt the door suddenly opened after all and the neighbour from the third floor came out onto the landing. I said that I'd come to visit the apartment on the second floor, but he told me the occupants had been taken away during a raid the previous morning. I'd obviously been lucky not to have been around at the time.

That was the moment when – for the second time – I decided to go and turn myself in at the theatre, as my situation was becoming more and more constrained and uncertain. My uncle and aunt's upstairs neighbour could clearly tell what was going on because he said that it might not be such a crazy idea to hide in my uncle's apartment, since it had been crossed off the list and they wouldn't come back there again. I thought about it but I didn't dare. I thanked him and quickly went on my way because it was all getting too much for me again. Fear, loneliness and panic completely overwhelmed my mind and I wandered around vacantly for a while.

I passed our house and looked up, but nothing had changed. Puls, the removal firm that emptied the homes of the deported, obviously hadn't visited yet. That meant all our things were still there – but I couldn't bring myself to go in. I felt hungry again and remembered my money. Couldn't I just buy something you didn't need a food coupon for? But I didn't dare ask anyone to give me change for a guilder for fear of attracting attention: a child with a whole guilder would look suspicious. While I was mulling over how best to tackle the problem, I arrived on Waterlooplein and saw someone my father often used to visit, and whom I therefore also knew. He gave me change for my guilder and of course asked after my father. I told him he was at home and didn't dare say anything more.

By now I was so scared and suspicious that I could no longer bring myself to board a train to Hoevelaken. I had lost my support and anchor, my driving force: my father. He always gave me confidence; he told me what to do and how I should act. He was always there. Now I had to do everything on my own initiative. And although I had the initiative, I lacked the resolve. It was all just too much for a 13-year-old boy.

Without my realising it, my feet had brought me closer and closer to the theatre, but the nearer I got to Plantage Middenlaan, the more I dawdled. It was the same way I used to walk to school: like a boy who had to go, but didn't want to. At Nieuwe Herengracht I turned off towards Amstelstraat and followed Reguliersbreestraat towards the Munt, where I sat down on a doorstep and stared into space for a long time. What now? I still didn't have the faintest idea, so I just got up and started walking again. I spotted a house on the Singel that I had often visited with my father to see Mr and Mrs Bijl. I walked past it but didn't dare ring the bell. I think by that point I no longer had the nerve to do anything at all. After walking on a little way, however, I turned back and looked up at the first floor, hoping to catch a glimpse of somebody. But there was no sign of life. I walked on to Koningsplein, engulfed by waves of fear. Once again I headed back and looked up, but once again I saw no one.

Dejectedly, I walked away for the last time, but then I literally bumped into Mr Bijl, who was on his way home. I stood rooted to the spot. The thing I had wanted so badly had happened, but the fear had clearly run too deep. I couldn't utter a word. Mr Bijl took my hand and ushered me up the stairs to his apartment. Mrs Bijl and her daughter Stella, who was the same age as me, were in the kitchen when we came in, and I burst into tears. It had probably all been too much for me.

I can't remember how long I sat there crying; I think it was quite a while. The family waited calmly. After a time I was able to speak again and in fits and starts I told the whole story; I didn't skip one second of the whole miserable adventure. They decided that I would stay with them for the time being at least, and that I would be perfectly fine sleeping on the sofa in the living room.

Mrs Bijl asked me to undress as she wanted to clean my clothes. Then she washed me in the kitchen, in such a kind and motherly way that I wasn't at all embarrassed. When I came back into the room all clean and wrapped in a dressing gown that belonged to my benefactors, there were some sandwiches waiting for me. I ate them and had just started playing a game with Stella when I heard Mr and Mrs Bijl urgently whispering in the kitchen. I tried to hear what was being said and couldn't catch anything, but I suspected, of course, that it was about me.

Gradually I began to calm down a little. I felt safe and comfortable, and for the first time in days I sensed that there was somebody around who really cared about me. At around six o'clock the table was laid for dinner. It was almost a festive occasion. I hadn't had much to eat over the last few days, let alone a cooked dinner. I started to feel a lot better and soon felt drowsy and tired. After dinner they made my bed. Mrs Bijl told me I'd better get some sleep as it would be good for me. It was still early and I didn't really want to, though I didn't say so, of course. But she was right, because I can't remember anything about the rest of that evening or night, so I must have fallen asleep straight away.

The next morning I woke up early and looked around in a daze. Where was I? Then the events of the previous day came back to me. I could hear noises in the kitchen, but didn't dare to stir. Everything was so peaceful and seemed so unreal. When Mrs Bijl crept into the room I quickly closed my eyes. I didn't know what to do. I'd never spent the night with strangers; we only ever stayed with family, with our uncles and aunts. When I cautiously opened my eyes, I found myself looking straight into the laughing face of Stella. 'I thought you'd never wake up,' she said. All of a sudden she had a new playmate, and she was very keen to make the most of me! I couldn't get up while she was there as I was in my underwear, and a boy really couldn't get out of bed like that. I had no idea how to handle this; I wasn't used to being around girls as at home we were all boys.

Luckily Mrs Bijl came in and saved me from my awkward situation. She put all my laundered and ironed clothes on the chair, and after I'd washed and dressed, I went into the kitchen for breakfast. I was allowed to eat as much as I liked, and believe me, I certainly did!

After breakfast Stella and I were given a bag and told to go shopping. I looked at the girl's coat and saw that there was no star on it. Once we got outside, I asked her about it and she told me that she didn't have to wear one because although her father was Jewish, her mother was not, which meant she wasn't one either as far as the Germans were concerned. By the time we got back Mr Bijl was home again. He told me he'd tried to find lodgings for me, but without success. Only then did I realise that I couldn't remain here. I had instantly made this safe haven my own and assumed I could just stay with them, without anyone giving me any reason to think so. I hadn't had the nerve to ask either, and nobody had brought it up. I would have only a few days of warmth and security in this loving home on the Singel, and then disaster would engulf me once more. I was certain of it.

Over supper that evening, Mr Bijl told me gently that in a few days they would have to go out of town to visit family, and he casually asked if I knew of anywhere else I could stay. I turned ice-cold and felt numb. I replied in a dull voice that I would go and stay with relatives. I don't know how I came up with that lie so quickly, but I wanted to spare these people my grim feelings.

During my last weekend there I made the most of the luxurious conditions. What a difference from roaming the streets and sleeping in air raid shelters!

When Monday morning arrived, we had breakfast and I stood up to say goodbye. They gave me some food to take with me and Mr Bijl even gave me some money with the words, 'You never know.' The tears only came once I'd left and gone round the corner. It is impossible to explain how I felt just then.

Luckily the weather was fine, and I walked towards Central Station. I was debating whether to go to Hoevelaken after all, but what if I turned up and they had no room for me? What then? My decision was made: I would go not to Hoevelaken, but to Uncle Joop on Haarlemmerstraat. He might have heard news of my father. That possibility hadn't occurred to me over the last few days, but now I was on my own again. I was evidently so preoccupied with myself that I hardly thought of my family at all, which is obviously unimaginable.

When I arrived at Uncle Joop's he had several customers in his shop, and he gestured for me to quickly go through to the back. He was worried someone would see me and wonder what I was doing there, as he explained later. Lena was there again and she wanted to know where I'd been all that time. I just made something up because I was getting quite good at telling fibs. I knew how to talk a lot without actually saying anything. Never tell anyone where you've really been or what you've been up to; that was nobody's business, that was dangerous. You learned that on the street soon enough.

When Uncle Joop came in he looked at me questioningly. Before I could say anything he asked me if I had heard from my father at all, and I told him I hadn't. Well, neither had he. I'd known that all along really, like having a sort of radar that tells you things, but still I had that 'frozen' feeling inside again when I heard it.

★ ★ ★

After the war, I was told by people who had been on the same train as my father that he was shot dead during the journey, and that didn't surprise me. He had always vowed that he would never just let them cart him off. He would choose his own time to die.

★ ★ ★

Uncle Joop thought I should leave Amsterdam and said he would try to find an address for me. He told me to call on him again in a few days, but he added that when I came in I should walk straight to the back of the shop. I didn't really understand why. After all, there was nothing suspicious about me. Who would think anything of it if I walked in?

7

By the time I left Uncle Joop's shop it was already three o'clock and I went back to my old neighbourhood near Nieuwmarkt. What was it Uncle Bernhard's neighbour had said? It should be fine to spend the night in your uncle and aunt's apartment as they've already been taken away, so the Germans won't look there again. Maybe he was right. Surely they wouldn't go back? I planned to ring the bell and then head straight up to the second floor.

On the way back to Koningsstraat I met Ina, one of the girls who had worked for Uncle Bernhard in his toy workshop. She came straight up to me and started asking all sorts of questions – something I was used to by now. She was so preoccupied with my plight that we didn't even notice when another raid started. I was gripped with panic and wanted to run away, but she almost barked at me that I should stay with her. That brought me back to my senses and I meekly did as I was told. She set off towards Nieuwmarkt. By the time we arrived, there were rolls of barbed wire at the entrance to the Jewish quarter again.

Ina walked straight up to the soldiers on duty with a smile on her face and pointed with her finger to indicate that she needed to pass through. The German looked at her, saw a lovely head of bushy blonde hair and no star, and smiled back. Then he pushed the barbed wire aside for us. Ina held my hand and strode on, self-assured and silent, and I obediently followed her. She walked down Oudezijds Achterburgwal to the Dam. When we got there, I tentatively asked her where we were going. 'To my place,' she answered. I walked on, feeling numb, unable quite to grasp what had just happened. I couldn't take it all in any more. But I had learned that in some situations, a lot of unpleasantness can be avoided by acting boldly, even audaciously.

The rest of the walk passed me by like a dream. When we reached Raadhuisstraat, Ina stopped in front of a shop called Wittenburg that sold party products. She opened the door that led to the apartments above it and went up the stairs, with me trailing behind her. A door opened on the fourth floor and another girl appeared. She asked Ina where she'd been all that time but Ina gestured for her not to pose too many questions. The girl looked me up and down and then gave me a friendly smile. Once we were inside, they put me in a chair and sat down on either side of me. Then they started peppering me with queries. What was I supposed to say now?

In the end I decided to tell them the truth, just like I had with Mr and Mrs Bijl. That seemed much easier than having to invent things all the time, and, besides, why shouldn't I tell the truth? If Ina had meant me any harm, she wouldn't have taken me with her, would she now? Once I'd told them more or less everything, she pulled me close. Her cheeks were wet and a moment later we were both sobbing. I still remember how much good it did me to tell someone the whole story and then feel a pair of arms around me. I suddenly felt immensely safe.

The other girl, Suze, laid the table and a quarter of an hour later we had dinner. Once we'd finished, my rescuer said that I should stay the night with them. For a while I'd actually forgotten that I might have had to spend another night in a stairwell or an air raid shelter. They took me to a small side room with just a single bed, a little table and a chair, but to me it was like a room in a five-star hotel. After I undressed and lay down in my new bed, I was told that I mustn't leave the room under any circumstances until the next morning, no matter what I heard, and even if I thought that she and Suze were still up. There really was nothing to fear, she assured me; if I stayed in my room I'd be completely safe.

I soon fell asleep, but was woken by loud voices and laughter. After a while I realised that the voices were speaking German. I lay still, as if I were paralysed. Had they betrayed me? Everything went quiet for a moment, but then I heard more German and lots of laughter. I couldn't understand a word. The noise didn't stop, but nothing happened either; the door didn't open and no Germans appeared. I was wide awake by now and fear was roaring through my body. Then I couldn't stand it any longer. I got up, opened the door a little, and peeped through the crack into the room opposite, where I saw part of a bed and a chair with a German uniform hanging over it.

★ ★ ★

In those days, as a 13-year-old boy, you couldn't take in such a situation, let alone make sense of it. It was quite a few years before I understood what had gone on in that room.

★ ★ ★

I quickly shut the door. I considered getting dressed and sneaking out, but I didn't dare. So I went back to my bed and lay still, staring at the ceiling. Eventually I must have fallen asleep again, because I only woke up when someone very softly said my name and stroked my hair. When I opened my eyes I found myself looking into the smiling face of a woman. What a wonderful way to wake up! I got up, washed and dressed. Then I was given a sandwich and a cup of tea with lots of sugar. Once we'd finished eating, Ina told me that she and Suze had to go to work, so I couldn't stay here during the day, but that I was welcome to come back at six to eat and sleep. I said I would, and I really meant it. But later that day I remembered the previous night and I decided not to go back after all. The terror was too fresh in my memory.

★ ★ ★

Of course I should have gone back. I think it would have been the safest place for me. Those Germans had better things to do than pay any notice to a little boy whom they knew nothing about. But sadly I didn't realise that at the time.

★ ★ ★

A week or two later, as I was walking along Spuistraat, someone tapped me on the shoulder. I felt my face go deathly pale and I froze, not daring to look back. Only when I heard a girl's voice did the blood flow back to my cheeks. I turned around to find myself looking at Nel. Nel often came to see us at home, but to this day I don't know what for. I only knew her face and her first name – nothing more. Once again I was faced with the usual barrage of questions, though I was getting better at dodging them. We talked a little, and then she suggested I should come home with her. She lived a little further along on Spuistraat above a well-known greengrocer's, whose owner everyone knew was a staunch member of the Dutch Nazi party.

Sitting at their big dining table, Nel began to tell her mother the details of my predicament. Nel had quickly figured out what was going on, so I just kept quiet. Without asking me, she and her mother decided that I would spend the night with them. That evening I was treated to a hearty meal, and after having a wash in the kitchen, I saw that they'd even made a bed for me in the meantime, ready for me to crawl straight in. I think I fell asleep as soon as my head touched the pillow.

After breakfast the following morning I went out again, but they made me promise to come back that evening to stay another night. Life was getting a bit easier now. On the third evening I was walking down Spuistraat on the way to my new lodgings when I saw two men approaching on bicycles. Don't ask me why, but I suddenly had a feeling something wasn't right and I quickly walked on. When I came back an hour later and rang the bell, Nel flew down the stairs and told me that two men had come looking for me. Luckily there was nothing in the house to suggest I'd been there. Evidently my survival instinct was starting to get pretty sharp.

After that I went back to sleeping in stairwells and air raid shelters for a while. If I slept in a stairwell, I would always choose the top flight of stairs leading to the attic because no one ever went up there at night, and I always made sure to leave again very early in the morning. By this time I was starting to look like a real tramp. My shoes were worn through, my clothes were filthy, and I must have smelled pretty bad. At first I'd tried to look fairly presentable, but after a while I gave up. It was pointless anyway. Finding food was much more important, and I was getting better and better at nicking it.

One night I decided to sleep in the apartment on Koningsstraat after all, but it turned out to be the worst decision I would make in the whole war. I rang the bell for the neighbour on the third floor, who luckily pulled the string to open the front door himself. When he looked down the stairs and saw me, he just nodded and quickly vanished back into his apartment. I went up to the second floor and pushed open the door to the apartment. As far as I knew, nobody else had seen me enter. Everything was just as my uncle and aunt had left it, which meant that Puls hadn't been here yet. I checked the whole apartment but stayed away from the windows for fear of being seen. I didn't switch on the lights either, although I now wonder if anyone would have paid much attention. There was mouldy bread in the bread bin, but nothing else to eat. Luckily I'd got my hunger well under control over the previous few days; I felt less and less need for food. My grandfather always said, 'Gluttons aren't born, they're made', and I think my stomach was starting to adjust to the situation. After wandering around the apartment for a while I decided it was best to go to sleep. I lay down in the same bed from which my mother and Mr Kroon had woken me up, but I didn't care. I was so exhausted that I fell asleep immediately.

When I woke up the next morning it was already light and I noticed that it was busy outside. I could hear a lot of people running around and shouting, but I had no idea what was going on in the street. There was a strange sound in the distance that I'd never heard before. I lay still and listened as it came closer. Then I went cold as a corpse as I realised that there was a vehicle with a loudspeaker in the street below, and that a German voice was shouting, '*Alle Juden müssen sich reisefertig machen*' – 'All Jews must prepare for departure'.

I didn't speak German, but I knew damned well that this was a round-up. For an instant my brain seized up and my heart skipped a beat. I felt like a rat in a trap. Then I flew out of bed and dressed at lightning speed. I tried to think what to do. I'd been trained at home to leave the building via the roof, so I stormed up the stairs and found a wooden ladder on the attic landing. I climbed up as fast as I could, pushed open a wooden trapdoor and stuck my head through the opening. All I could see was a chimney, so I clambered onto the roof. I had no idea which way to go. I took a step forward to work out where Nieuwmarkt was, and found myself staring down the barrel of a German rifle.

A soldier was standing on the roof of the Flessenman building, less than eighty metres away. At that same moment he saw me and I heard him scream, '*Gehe nach unten oder ich schieße*' – 'Go back down or I'll shoot'. I dashed round to the safe side of the chimney and virtually dived back through the trapdoor and down the four flights of stairs. Shaking like a leaf and gasping for breath, I stood in the corridor behind the front door. I could barely control my legs. The fear was almost strangling me. Then my eye fell on a hatch in the wall with a sliding door. The owner of the butcher's,

Mr Velleman, had lived above the premises for a while and had used this as a quick route to work. I opened the little door, went through into the shop and closed it behind me as best I could.

The ceiling had exposed beams, like many shops in Amsterdam do, and there was a large built-in refrigerator at the back of the room that reached all the way up to the beams. I climbed on top of it and squeezed my skinny body into the small gap under the ceiling. I had only just managed to hide when I heard boots running up the stairs. Then there were footsteps over my head, yelling, cupboards opening and slamming shut again. The whole house was being searched from top to bottom, and when they came down the stairs again, I held my breath. Even today I can still hear them shouting, '*Hier ist keiner*' – 'Nobody here'. They clearly hadn't spotted the little doorway on the ground-floor corridor. It wasn't very obvious; it got a bit lost amid the wall panels.

The Germans left the building and all was quiet again, but I stayed safely in my hiding place for the time being. I have no idea how long I lay there before I decided to take my chances. After I'd climbed out, I had to dust myself down because my clothes were covered in muck. I left the shop via the little connecting door and found myself standing in the corridor of my uncle and aunt's apartment block once again. I thought of my father. He would have rested his hand on my head. That gesture always filled me with pride; to me, it meant something like, 'You did well there, my boy.' I knelt down by the door and peeped through the letterbox to see if there was anything still happening outside, but all seemed calm.

I stepped tentatively onto the street and started walking towards Nieuwmarkt. My heart almost stopped at what I saw there. The place was teeming with policemen in green and black, and wherever you looked there were people with backpacks and suitcases. Trams were riding up and down Sint Antoniesbreestraat with loudspeakers on the roof, constantly repeating the words, '*Alle Juden müssen sich reisefertig machen*'.

By now, my brain was working perfectly again and I rapidly weighed up what I had to do. I still couldn't believe that nobody would pay any attention to me. I was a boy of 13 with blond hair, blue eyes and no star – you couldn't get more German than that. Yet I had the feeling that every Kraut was looking at me with suspicion, and I expected to be grabbed by the collar at any moment and thrown onto one of the trams. But nothing of the sort happened. I walked through the streets of the Jewish quarter and saw the most terrible things. Truly I will never be able to forget that day; it will always be with me.

Trams and cars were crammed full of people ready to be deported. Every street was blocked with barriers covered in barbed wire and guarded by soldiers. Nobody was allowed in or out of the Jewish quarter, whether they had a star or not. Even a sweet, smiling blonde girl wouldn't have stood a chance. It was an enormous trap – the biggest raid I had ever seen. And I was right in the middle of it.

Eventually I found myself on Utrechtsestraat, but the Germans hadn't overlooked any exits here either. In the distance, I could see that the junction between Utrechtsestraat and Frederiksplein was heavily guarded. My fear drove

In a guarded tram, Jews are transported to Muiderpoort station.
(Beeldbank WO2/Resistance Museum, Amsterdam/K.F.H. Bönnekamp)

me on, and as it became clearer and clearer that I had little chance of getting out, I got terribly upset. But in truth I was in no danger at all.

At the Frederiksplein end of Utrechtsestraat there was a shop selling military and naval uniforms. Lots of officers went there; I knew that because a girl who used to work at our house had a fiancé whose uniform had been made there. During the occupation you could buy German uniforms there from the same people, especially uniforms for the Dutch Nazi party. As I stood looking through the shop window, not knowing what else to do, my eye was caught by some Dutch Nazi party badges that cost fifteen cents each. I stepped inside and bought one. The woman in the shop congratulated me on my choice and even went to the trouble of pinning it to my coat.

Back outside, I was gripped by a terrible sense of shame, but my reason prevailed and I walked on with my head held high. Once again I felt my father's hand on my head. With the courage of desperation, I walked straight up to a soldier standing by the barbed wire – one from the *Grüne Polizei*, they were always better than the Dutch police – and proudly showed him my badge. Then the miracle happened: the soldier, who was busy talking to another soldier, barely glanced at me and made a space between two barriers to let me through. I walked on as if I was in a trance and only came to my senses a long way down Van Woustraat. I'd escaped!

I arrived at the Amstel Canal. With a sense of revulsion, but also a feeling that I'd been reborn – that I'd been given a second chance – I took off the badge and dropped it over the railing of the bridge into the water.

8

Now I had both feet back on the ground, but where to go from here? The neighbourhood I found myself in wasn't familiar territory. Then I had an idea. I was very near Van Ostadestraat, which was where I'd visited a woman during one of the first raids to tell her that her husband was safe at our house. I decided to go there; maybe she could put me up for a few days.

When I arrived at the address, no one answered the door. I decided to walk around for a while, as they might have been out shopping. After three-quarters of an hour I tried again, but then a neighbour came out and said that no one lived there any more. I asked her – very stupidly – if she knew where they'd moved to. The woman looked at me sadly and said that the Germans had taken them away. I was stunned. Until then I'd thought that only happened in my old neighbourhood.

I hurried back to my own familiar surroundings and saw that the huge raid was over. Even so, I decided not to spend the night there. I had to choose between Raadhuisstraat, the Singel or the air raid shelter yet again. Raadhuisstraat seemed the most appealing option, but those Germans in the house made me opt for the Singel, assuming that was still possible. At five o'clock I turned up at the Bijls' place, where they welcomed me with open arms; apparently they'd been waiting for me for days, worried about my fate.

I had completely lost count; I had no idea how long I'd been living on the streets by that point. The only thing I knew was that it was Sunday again, because I'd heard the church bells that morning and because all life seemed to have vanished from the streets.

★ ★ ★

Before the war it was the city's Jewish residents who brought Sundays to life, because their shops stayed open and the Jewish Corner (the market in Uilenburg) attracted people from all over Amsterdam. Now the market was gone, the shops were closed, the area seemed dead.

★ ★ ★

After dinner they were eager to tell me their news. At first I thought they knew something about my father, but that hope was soon dashed. Mr Bijl had found someone who could find me a hiding place on a farm, and that same evening he'd go to see if he could find the man. I could stay at their place until everything was arranged.

Next day Stella and I went to the shops with her mother. They bought me a new pair of socks and it felt like my birthday. To get a new pair of socks from a stranger, just like that, was very special. What made the day even more memorable was that I discovered I could be attracted to a girl. I was finally becoming a teenager and my hormones were making themselves known. For one reason or another girls seemed to have a lot to do with it.

After two days at the house on the Singel, a man – whose name was not mentioned – paid a visit in the afternoon. That wasn't strange; during the war people often didn't have names, and if a name was given it was mostly a false one. After fifteen minutes he left again, saying he would be back in a few days. About three days later Mr Bijl said that the man would be coming to visit again and that he was going to take me with him. I mustn't ask any questions, just do as I was told, and all would be well.

I didn't really like that. I was beginning to feel pretty independent and to act like it too, and now I had to meekly follow someone else's orders again. The thought of that made me feel less safe. Maybe I was the best judge of what I should or shouldn't do. That wasn't such an illogical notion: day after day I'd had to make decisions that were often of vital importance, and I was still here, so by now I had total confidence in myself. Why should I suddenly trust a complete stranger again?

But despite all my misgivings, he came to collect me. The Bijls said their goodbyes and I was handed a red tin with some sandwiches in it. Mrs Bijl told me to be sure to keep it safe, as she would like me to return it to her after the war was over. That would be wonderful, she said, and smiled. I loved it when she gave me a big warm hug and a kiss on both cheeks, but I felt less comfortable when Stella also gave me a kiss and asked if I would come to visit again some time. All I could think to do was give a mindless nod.

I walked silently alongside the man towards Central Station. His legs were too long for me, so I had trouble keeping up with him, and he didn't say a word the whole way, which made me feel uneasy. But right in front of the station he looked at me.

'If someone asks you where we're going, you tell them we're on our way to see an aunt,' he instructed me. I couldn't have said more than that anyway because I had no idea what was going to happen to me or where I was going.

We took our seats on the train and I thought of Doortje. It wasn't so long ago that I had taken her away, and now I was being taken away by a stranger whose name I didn't even know. I wasn't afraid, but I felt very sad and lonely.

The journey seemed endless. Now and then the man looked at me and smiled. He was trying to be friendly, but without much success. He was probably afraid of getting caught, or maybe I was the first child he'd had to take to a hiding place. I would never know the true reason. At last the train stopped and we got off. Though we'd walked quickly in Amsterdam, we now dawdled, so we obviously had plenty of time. After a while we came to a little wall; he sat me down on it and said I wasn't to move under any circumstances and that I had to wait quietly. At some point a woman would come by, shake my hand and tell me to come with her.

So there I was, alone, clutching my little red tin.

The man walked away, back to the station. I felt miserable and lonely and I wanted to cry like a baby, but I didn't have time for that because just then a woman came up to me, shook my hand and told me what a big boy I was. Nobody had ever managed to put me at ease so quickly and completely as that lady did. I was terribly happy to meet her. I probably felt just like a stray dog would if someone talked to it kindly, gave it some food and said, 'Come on, you can sleep at my house tonight.'

She took me with her to a big house – a beautiful manor house with a large garden bordering on a small canal. I wouldn't have minded staying here for the rest of the war! There were lots of friendly people who didn't treat me like a waif. The lady of the house took me upstairs to a real bathroom – a huge room with a big bathtub in the middle that you could walk all the way round. She told me to undress while she ran the bath. For the first time in my life I didn't dare take off my underwear. To stand there naked in front of this strange woman was asking a bit much; I was a teenager now, after all.

But she handled it very considerately by saying she would just go out to fetch some clean underwear and in the meantime I could make myself comfortable in the lovely warm bath. It never occurred to me for a second at the time, but my underwear must have been too filthy to touch with a barge pole. After I got out of the bath, all fresh and clean, I had to get dressed in another room, where to my amazement I found a whole new set of clean clothes waiting for me.

I woke up early next morning, jumped out of bed and ran over to the window. My room was at the back of the house and faced the big garden. There was a man standing in one corner looking up. I still didn't know what was to become of me and I'd never seen the man before, so I immediately felt nervous and scared. Over time I'd become not only very cautious, but also suspicious. The man greeted me with a wave and went back to work. Was he really just the gardener?

I had no idea what time it was and didn't dare to leave the room, so I just sat and waited for someone to come. There were photographs in frames hanging on the wall and I started looking at each of them in turn. Many of the photos were of children, often gathered around the lady of the house. While I was looking at a picture with at least twenty people in it, she suddenly appeared next to me. I was so engrossed in the photo that I hadn't even heard her come in and it gave me quite a start. She apologised for making me jump and said she'd thought I was still asleep. Seeing my interest in the picture, she told me who all the people in it were. She had five children who were all married. One of the couples was still living with her as they hadn't yet managed to find a place of their own.

She led me to the bathroom and on the way asked me to call her Auntie Bep, as that would make it easier for us to talk. Once I'd washed and dressed, she took me downstairs. A table was set in the kitchen, heaped with what looked to me like a lavish amount of food.

'If you're really hungry you can start eating now, but if not we'll wait till everybody's here,' said Auntie Bep. I said I could easily wait, even though I was starving.

Suddenly people came into the kitchen from all directions, including the man from the garden. When he saw me he came up to me and held out his hand. My whole hand disappeared in his for a moment and I hoped I'd get it back unscathed. And so the gardener turned out to be the man of the house. He made a remark that I didn't understand, at least not just then. 'So, we've got another one?'

I was in a halfway house.

That day was one big party; lots and lots of people dropped in and everyone was terribly friendly to me. At no point did I feel like I was in a bizarre situation. I took things for granted and completely trusted these people, without being able to say exactly why I felt I could drop my guard.

★ ★ ★

In Amsterdam I weighed up everybody I met and found them wanting far too often. In hindsight I was often amazed at how quickly I was able to adjust to new situations, be they pleasant or miserable. Everything quickly became the new normal. During that time I became a real chameleon, and in a way I've remained so ever since.

★ ★ ★

Nobody talked about me; it was as if I belonged there. It didn't occur to me for a second that I might have to leave again soon; I had no idea what a halfway house was exactly. You might say I was burying my head in the sand, but I didn't want to think of anything beyond this safe haven. The day passed without any shocking events, and that was something so special for me that I cherished every moment.

That evening Auntie Bep wasn't at home; I was alone with the man of the house and a girl, but everything was the same as before. When it began to get dark the girl said it might be a good idea for me to go to bed. I would have liked to stay up until Auntie Bep came back, but I didn't dare ask, so I followed her up the beautiful staircase with its curved banisters to the room where I slept. Once I'd got undressed and climbed into bed, the girl came back to check that all was well. It was just like how I imagined a grand hotel to be! She carefully tucked me in, bent over me with a smile and gave me a kiss. That made a deep impression on me. A feeling of warmth and security washed over me like a big wave – so pleasant and lovely. How can I describe what went on in my mind and what I felt? Even now it's beyond me. I snuggled down under the blankets and fell asleep, satisfied and almost even happy.

The next morning I woke up early again. I wasn't used to long nights any more and a little voice told me something was going to happen. It wasn't a good feeling. Auntie Bep's absence the previous night had unsettled me more than I'd realised. I wandered round the room a bit but didn't dare leave it. The house was very quiet and I couldn't see anyone in the garden either, so I went back to bed. I must have fallen asleep again because I was woken up by someone very gently stroking my face. When I opened my eyes I saw Auntie Bep's face, and that immediately restored my faith in the future.

After washing and dressing, I went downstairs to the big cosy kitchen where everybody was already having breakfast. I was a little embarrassed for making them wait, but no one mentioned it. Everything seemed so cheerful again that I soon lost the bad feeling I'd woken up with.

Once breakfast was over, I joined my host in the garden and tried to help. He gave me a basket and said I could pick runner beans because Auntie Bep needed them for lunch. I felt proud standing with my little knife amongst the tall stakes and cutting off the biggest beans. What did a boy from the city know about picking beans?

It was delightful in the garden and I was disappointed when it was suddenly midday and we went in to eat. That was another thing I'd already got used to. I still remember how wonderful it all was. I wasn't used to country life – to losing myself in nature and being at one with it. I revelled in the freedom and in not having to worry, but most of all I enjoyed being with these kind and sweet people. I couldn't have wished for more.

The day went by far too quickly. At half past five we went in for dinner, and the man of the house cautiously began to ask questions, but Auntie Bep said – and this remark stayed with me for a very long time – that it was better to know as little as possible. He looked at her and I saw an expression full of pity cloud his face for an instant. Their eyes held each other briefly and then the moment passed.

After dinner Auntie Bep went into the garden and asked me to join her. There was nothing I liked better. We were standing by the canal when she looked at me and told me I couldn't stay with her. She had found an address for me where I would have a wonderful time and where I could stay until the end of the war, if all went well. 'It might not be as big a house as the one we have here, but the people who live there are very kind and lovely. They don't have children themselves and they would love to have a boy come and stay with them.'

The announcement hit me like a blow with a sledge-hammer. I stared at the ground, utterly crushed, and felt myself turning all cold and stiff. I'd been convinced that I could stay here with Auntie Bep. I could feel my lip trembling and I bravely tried to hold back the tears, but to no avail. Auntie Bep took my face between her hands and pulled me close. How many children did she have to console like that? Children who, just like me, had believed that they could stay with her. Who had all been welcomed in the same way, who had all slept in the same room, in the same big bed, and who had then had to say goodbye in the same abrupt fashion, on their way to the next unknown address.

And how often must this woman have suppressed her own tears?

★　★　★

Anyone who did things like this during the war must have had a big and warm heart, that's for sure. Besides all the stress this woman must have endured, to some extent she must also have grown attached to the children she so lovingly cared for, only to have to let them go again after a few days to make room for the next one, and the next, and the next.

After the war I tried so many times to figure out where that house was, but I never succeeded. I simply have no idea where I spent those few wonderful days.

★　★　★

Auntie Bep put her arm around me and we went back indoors. She made a pot of tea straight away and gave me a mug and a piece of cake. She tried to put me at ease again, but it didn't work.

When it got dark she took me upstairs for the night, and once I was tucked in she sat down on the edge of the bed and silently took my hand. There was no need for words; everything spoke for itself. Once again I was overwhelmed with fear of the unknown. She stayed with me until I fell asleep, so I didn't see or hear her leave. That spared me a lot of tears that night.

When I woke up the next morning I lay quietly, reflecting on the immediate past. Sleeping in stairwells and air raid shelters, then in a comfortable bed again or just on a sofa in a cosy living room, and now once again I faced an unknown future. Where would I end up next? Maybe somewhere worse, but it might also be even better. It was a good thing that we didn't know everything in advance.

I heard noises downstairs, but just as I was about to get out of bed, the door flew open. Auntie Bep came in smiling and said I didn't have to get dressed just yet. She was going to run the bath so I could go to my new home all fresh and clean. I suddenly thought of my mother. It was strange how rarely I thought of my family. I think I was so preoccupied with myself that there was no room for anyone else.

Eventually I came downstairs and took a seat at the table. It felt like everyone was looking at me with sad faces, but that was probably just my imagination. During breakfast a slim, petite girl came in. She had shoulder-length blonde hair and was wearing a raincoat made of Egyptian linen. I'd heard so much about different textiles at home that I recognised these things straight away. After shaking everyone's hands, she came up to me and looked at me with her big blue eyes, smiling. Taking my hand in hers, she said, 'So, we're going out together today.' Without pausing for breath, she added, 'Everyone will think you're my little brother; you've got blond hair and blue eyes too, and you're not too tall either. That makes things much easier!' Then she told me she wanted to catch the bus at quarter past nine.

After that everything moved very quickly. I'd hardly swallowed my last mouthful before Auntie Bep got to her feet. She'd put some clothes in a travel bag, and to avoid making things worse than they already were, she said goodbye very quickly and we were out in the street before I knew it.

9

It was a five-minute walk to the bus stop and as soon as we'd taken our seats, the bus drove off. As it rounded the corner, I turned back for a last look. Then I glanced at the pretty girl beside me and her friendly face. I was very taken with her and her fresh, youthful beauty. That was a sign I was growing up, war or no war. She chattered incessantly, though she didn't really say anything. She explained that we would have to change buses again, and I didn't ask where we were going. I'd learned better by now.

After about twenty minutes the bus stopped in a small village square where another bus stood waiting. German soldiers were there to check the passengers as they changed buses, but the girl assured me that nothing would happen and there was nothing to worry about. She showed her identity card to one soldier and he smiled at her. She smiled back and we carried on. I was completely ignored. For the first time I wasn't afraid of that uniform either. In these rural parts, where things were quieter and friendlier, it seemed the soldiers were different too. As it turned out, that was only true of the Germans.

After half an hour we came to a halt at a little church and everyone got off. Hand in hand we walked through narrow old streets to a tree with a bicycle leaning against it. The girl unlocked the bike and told me to sit on the rear carrier. 'Keep your feet well away from the spokes so we don't have any accidents,' she warned. Then we cycled out of the village and I saw a sign saying Ommen. I looked around, savouring the view. All I could see were sprawling fields of rye, as she told me. The paths were so narrow that I could reach out and touch the stalks. I had no idea where Ommen was, and I didn't care either. I was enjoying the beauty of nature and the silence, breathing the wonderful country air deep into my lungs, and I stopped worrying about my friend having to do the hard work of cycling down these tracks. After about a quarter of an hour the path got wider and we entered the yard of a tiny white farmhouse, surrounded by grain fields. We got off the bike and the girl laid it on the ground.

Once again I was about to confront a new, unfamiliar and possibly unpleasant situation. What kind of people were waiting for me? Would I like them? And, most importantly, would they like me?

The front door opened directly into the living room, which was a small space furnished with the bare essentials. In the middle stood a table laid with large white bowls and spoons. There were four places set out, so we were obviously expected. The girl seemed to know the people well because she began to talk with the man at length in a dialect that I didn't understand. When the girl saw that they were counting on her to join us for the meal, she apologised and said she couldn't stay long. She left after ten minutes. When she said goodbye she told me that she would come to visit soon because she lived close by. She must have been able to tell from my face that I wasn't happy to see her leave so quickly, but she assured me that I'd feel settled within a few days. I watched through the window as she cycled off until she disappeared from view.

The woman of the house told me her name was Mrs Zwaal and asked me to come to the table. Once the three of us were seated, Mr Zwaal asked me if I prayed before eating. I replied that I didn't. Without saying anything more, he folded his hands and the woman followed suit. He prayed out loud and very quickly, but even if he'd spoken slowly it still wouldn't have meant anything to me; I couldn't understand a word of their dialect. After the prayer, a grey pan full of some kind of porridge appeared on the table. I put a spoonful in my mouth but could barely swallow. It was horrible. I had to force myself to finish my serving. And precisely because I found it so disgusting, I ate very quickly to get it over and done with, just like I used to do at home with cod liver oil. But because I'd emptied my bowl so quickly, the woman thought I'd enjoyed it and in her kindness she heaped another big dollop onto my plate. There was plenty of rye to go round!

At some point – I don't know why – I looked out the window and saw someone in the distance cycling towards us very quickly.

Fate had struck again.

When the woman reached the house, she threw her bike to the ground, flung the door open and yelled, 'That boy has to go right now – they're coming!'

I sat and stared straight ahead, paralysed, unable to take in what was happening around me. In a matter of seconds, the small, peaceful little room was transformed into a madhouse. The man grabbed my arm, pushed me out through the front door and pointed the way I should go.

I ran through a field, crouching as I went. Luckily the rye was so tall that I was completely hidden as long as I stayed hunkered down. I ran as fast as I could for several minutes until I heard the sound of cars approaching. When the engines fell silent, I stood stock-still. What in heaven's name was happening? Very carefully, I peered over the stalks at the house, and what I saw there was horrifying.

★ ★ ★

It turned out that there was a camp near the house belonging to the National Socialist Motor Corps, or NSKK – a Dutch elite force that had been specially created by the Germans, but which some Dutchmen collaborated with all too eagerly. These paramilitary policemen were part of a group of pro-German officers who were specially trained for this sort of dirty work. They were the ones who so obligingly dragged Jews out of their houses and put them on transports.

★ ★ ★

There were two white armoured cars in the yard, and men in black uniforms were running in and out of the farmhouse. I saw a window open on the upper floor and two men stared out. I immediately withdrew deeper into the safety of the tall rye. When I looked again, I saw to my dismay that they were throwing the poor couple's belongings out of the windows. Blankets, sheets and all sorts of things that I couldn't make out from that distance were hurled out into the yard. They were hunting for me.

Someone must have seen me back in the village, and evidently there was only one house on this lane. Maybe people were already suspicious of the girl that brought me here, or maybe they'd recognised me as a fugitive going into hiding. I couldn't see any more movement in the house, but now I heard a voice somewhere outside shouting, 'He must be here somewhere. He can't have gone far!'

Then something happened that I'd only ever seen in films: they started shooting into the rye. I can still hear the rustling of the bullets through the stalks. The hunt was on, and the quarry was a 13-year-old Jewish boy.

I won't attempt to describe my fear – that's impossible. I couldn't move, even if I'd wanted to. Everything I did in this situation was pure instinct. There was no such thing as heroism. My brain stopped working. I went numb. I was so completely paralysed with fear that everything around me blurred: time, movement, life, everything ceased to exist. And then I fell asleep.

★ ★ ★

Years went by before I understood that I must have suffered a blackout. I spent so long racking my brains over how it was possible for me to calmly lie down and go to sleep like that.

★ ★ ★

When I came to, I knew that something had woken me up. Still hovering halfway between waking and sleep, I heard a dog barking, and when I listened intently, I could make out two or three dogs making a furious racket. Far off in the distance, I could just hear someone shout, 'I'll go this way.' Then I began to understand what was going on. They were hunting me with dogs! They obviously had to find me, at all costs. Was it a kind of sport for them, catching Jewish kids?

I had to get out of there. I crawled on my hands and knees over the rye fields, scraping my skin on the hard, dry ground and the broken stalks. My only thought was that I had to make sure they didn't see any movement. The barking went on and on. I didn't dare look around. Suddenly I came up against a river; I could go no further. I sat there paralysed. Wouldn't it have been more sensible simply to hand myself in at the Hollandsche Schouwburg? Was all this worth it? Imagine if they caught me now; I'd have to go on the transport by myself.

But there wasn't much time for such idle thoughts because I could still hear the dogs barking, although I couldn't quite make out where the sound was coming from. I took a decision. When I stood up, I couldn't see them, which meant they couldn't see me either. I could still reason that far, thank goodness. I kept walking along the stream until I spotted a small rowing boat. Without stopping to think, I got in and paddled to the other bank, where I found a long pole sticking out of the water and realised I was supposed to tie the boat to it.

I hardly dare say it, but at that point I started to find it all rather thrilling. I'd managed to avoid being caught by a bunch of big grown-up men! I had outwitted them all!

After crossing the river, I immediately dived back into the rye, but this time I made my way parallel to the water, heading downstream. However, when darkness fell, the fear returned and I lost heart again. There was nothing for it but to keep walking, and yet my legs were starting to give up. I had no idea what time it was, but after a while a church bell chimed eleven o'clock. Two things were clear to me: the church bells meant there was a village nearby, and in an hour's time it would be absolutely forbidden for me to be outside.

As a stranger, I couldn't show my face in the village, especially not after midnight. Dragging myself along – you couldn't call it walking any more – I suddenly reached a narrow lane and a large farmhouse. It was dark all around and I thought about hiding there, but the farm obviously had a dog as it started barking when it heard me.

Three men in uniform on bicycles suddenly appeared from behind a bend in the road, coming my way. I was so astonished, my heart pounding with fear, that all I managed to say was 'Good evening'. They cheerfully answered, 'And a good evening to you too,' and went on their way.

The absolute worst thing about that night was the drone of British bombers on their way to carry out raids on Germany. Of course, it felt good to hear that something was happening far above your head to give you some little hope for the future, but on that night I had two reasons to curse their presence. The anti-aircraft guns scared me – I was out in the open, exposed, and I didn't know where the shots were coming from. And the monotonous drone of the planes wore on my nerves too.

After I'd walked a long way on that road, something appalling happened. Suddenly there was an incredibly loud bang and a fountain of fire sprayed up into the air. I remember I had a vague notion that a tree had caught fire, but what had really happened was that a plane had been shot down and had hit the ground very close to me and burst into flames.

I didn't dare take another step. I didn't have much time to think in any case because cars were approaching from all directions and I could hear voices yelling in German. I dived into a dry ditch beside the road and lay still. I quickly covered myself with some leaves and then I think I really did fall asleep.

It was already getting light by the time I woke up. The innate peace and calm of my surroundings had returned. I climbed out of my ditch and quickly patted my back pocket to make sure my money was still there. It was, thank goodness, because I really needed it now. I smoothed down my clothes as best I could and set off.

Yet again, I was starting to get used to a new situation. I was recovering from shocks more and more quickly each time. I kept having to reassess my chances of survival, and that skill was becoming second nature. Fear would hit me hard each time, but my confidence was also growing. The fear was passing more quickly too; I couldn't afford to be afraid longer than was absolutely necessary.

A man driving a horse and cart approached from behind me. I wasn't sure what to do, but there wasn't much I could do because there was nowhere to turn off the road. When the man reached me, he reined the horse in and asked where I was going. Because I didn't know myself, I just told him I was on my way to catch the bus. He replied that I was in luck, since he was going to the village and could take me with him. Then he told me that a British fighter plane had been shot down that night, and the Germans had hauled the farmer's whole family out of bed and turned his house upside down looking for the pilot. He didn't know if they'd found him.

I expect the man was still so full of the previous night's events that it didn't even occur to him to ask me any questions. He must have been able to tell from my accent that I wasn't a local.

When we reached the village, he stopped his cart and told me where I could catch the bus. There was already a long queue of people waiting to go into town for the day. I joined at the back and nobody paid any attention to me. Everybody knew each other, and they had so much to talk about that I wasn't of any interest to them. As the queue gradually shortened, it turned a corner. I hadn't spotted anything amiss, but when I rounded the corner I realised why it was moving so slowly. There were two soldiers with rifles slung across their torsos standing by the door of the bus and asking every passenger: '*Ausweis?*' You didn't have to carry any papers until you were 15, but that didn't occur to me at the time. There were only three people in front of me, and for the umpteenth time I died a thousand deaths. Then it was my turn.

Without saying a word, the German put his hand on my back and cheerfully pushed me onto the bus. Of course he didn't ask me anything; I was still only a child, even though I didn't see it that way. When the driver asked me where I was going, I randomly said, 'To the station.'

I only began to calm down again once we were nearly at the station. I had to recharge my batteries for the next big leap.

The woman behind the counter asked me where I was going.

'Amsterdam,' I answered.

'Single or return?'

'Single.' She handed me my ticket, I put the change in my back pocket and enquired what time and from which platform the train would leave. On the platform I asked a guard where the Amsterdam train was and he laughed and pointed at the one right in front of my nose. I immediately boarded to prevent any questions. I had the compartment to myself, but I instinctively took a seat in the corner, near the door, always keen to have an escape route. After about ten minutes on my own, the door opened and a German soldier with a smart cap sat down directly opposite me. The whole compartment was empty, and yet he had chosen to sit right in front of me.

The platform suddenly got much busier. A lot of people were walking along the train, ready to board. The door opened again and two more Germans entered, and before I knew it, the whole carriage was full of Germans. I got very anxious and looked around me. I could see the notices on the windows, but I didn't know what they said: *Nur Wehrmacht* (Soldiers only).

At the time I thought things couldn't get any worse, but in hindsight I think it was the safest place I could be on the whole train. I wanted to leave the carriage, but I didn't dare; I was scared I would draw far too much attention to myself. Seeing a man in the distance with a snack trolley, I stood up, lowered the window and called out to him, even though I knew perfectly well that he couldn't hear me. As I pulled the leather strap again to close the window, pleased with the excuse I'd come up with to leave the carriage, a German soldier grabbed my arm. This is the end, I thought, but then he smiled at me, pushed me back into my seat in a friendly way, opened the window and gave an inimitable roar of the kind that only Germans can produce. The man came rushing up with his trolley of treats and the soldier asked me what I wanted. I answered in a small voice, 'Something to drink.' He asked for two bottles and paid the man. When I showed him my money he laughed and gestured for me to put it away.

Only when we left the station did I see a sign saying that we were in Deventer.

The German sat across from me all the way to Amsterdam, smiling at me from time to time. The journey seemed to take forever because the train kept stopping whenever British planes flew overhead. At the next station he asked me if I wanted another drink, or at least that's what I understood from his gestures. I vehemently shook my head. When we finally arrived in Amsterdam we stood up at the same time. In those days there was still quite a difference in height between the train and the platform; it used to be a bit of a climb. The soldier stood waiting for me, reached out and helped me down the steps. Then we each went our separate ways.

I'd seen more than enough Germans for a while.

It was only after I arrived in the station at Amsterdam that I started to wonder where to go next. On the train I'd been so preoccupied with the soldier opposite me that the question hadn't even occurred to me. I was still mulling it over when the number thirteen tram pulled up. The number on the front reminded me that we sometimes used to take that line to visit acquaintances on Jan Evertsenstraat. I remembered exactly where they lived, above a potato shop.

So there I was, making my way through Amsterdam again. It was a long ride to Jan Evertsenstraat and I was happy to be back in my home town, even though it was really the most dangerous place for me to be roaming around. The tram stop was right in front of the shop – I always recognised it from the crates of potatoes in the window – so I only had to walk a few steps.

I rang the bell, the door opened almost immediately, and I ran up the two flights of stairs. At the top, Mr De Lange was standing in his doorway looking at me as if I were a ghost. I walked into the apartment, but the man remained in the doorway as if he were expecting more people – maybe the rest of my family? When it became clear that no one else was with me, he came in and gave me a questioning look, and I immediately poured out my story. The whole family sat around the table staring at me. They were flabbergasted.

It wasn't a very coherent tale, of course. So much had happened in such a short space of time that now I was back in the normal world, I felt completely shaken up. While I was talking, Mrs De Lange was looking me up and down. Their daughter, who must have been about 18, got up to make tea and came back to the table with some food. Only then did I realise how tired and hungry I was. Nobody said a word; the three of them just sat and stared at each other. Mrs De Lange was the first to pull herself together after my incredible story. She thought I should have a wash first, and that it would be sensible for me to go to bed for a while and try to get some sleep. That would also give her time to try to get my clothes halfway clean. 'If that's still possible,' she added doubtfully. I accepted the offer eagerly, because I felt shattered of course, if only from the stress.

At around four o'clock I woke up and found myself wearing a pair of Mr De Lange's pyjamas, which were far too big for me. The daughter, Coby, said we could go and check if my clothes were dry. We went up a flight of stairs to a huge flat roof space that had been converted into a garden. It was truly magnificent, especially for that time. I drank it all in, completely forgetting my ridiculous over-sized pyjamas. Coby laughed, saying that we could easily spend quite a while up there.

My experiences had sharpened my instincts and I instantly knew that I'd found shelter again, but I didn't reply for fear that I might have got it wrong.

All three of them were terribly kind to me and the time I spent with them was wonderful. I went to bed at eleven and lay quietly for a while, looking at my surroundings and revelling in the luxury. I had already forgotten about the ditch of the previous night. I couldn't allow myself to think about yesterday; only today and, above all, tomorrow were important.

10

In the middle of the night I was brutally awoken. When I opened my eyes I saw two men. 'Get up, and quickly,' a voice snarled. When I wasn't quick enough one of them thumped my shoulder. They took me to the living room where I had to dress while they kept watch. Five minutes later they walked me out the door while the family looked on. Down in the street one of them said, 'So, you rotten Jew, try to run away now and we'll bloody well shoot you on the spot.'

I only partly took in what was happening. They clearly knew quite a lot about my past already, as I don't think they'd have made that remark about my running away otherwise.

I was taken to a police station – I think the one on Vespuccistraat, though I don't remember for sure. They pushed me through a door and I practically fell into the room. Two policemen came to 'take delivery' of me. They were told to put me in 'the pen' for the time being. I didn't immediately understand what that was, but it turned out to be a holding cell. The first two said they'd come to collect me later that day and would let them know when. And the policemen followed their orders. So there I was. Thirteen years old. In a cell. A whole morning passed without anything happening except that at one point I was brought something to eat. Nobody was horrible to me but no one was nice either. The strange thing was that I actually felt quite safe in that cell. The door was a barrier separating good from bad. As long as it stayed closed, I was safely tucked away and no one could hurt me.

Some time in the afternoon I was taken out of my cell to find two other men waiting for me. They took me to a car and told me to sit in the back. One of them got behind the wheel and the other took a seat next to me. We drove through Amsterdam. Neither of them said a word, not to me and not to each other. During the drive I felt remarkably calm. I'd been caught, which meant I didn't have to turn myself in. I no longer had to rack my brains about how to stay alive either. I resigned myself to whatever was about to happen.

We stopped in Paulus Potterstraat in front of a grand-looking house. First you had to climb some stone steps and then an imposing staircase that felt very much in keeping with the house. As I was taken upstairs I let my hand glide over the wonderful curlicued wooden banister. There was a bend in the staircase, followed by another five or so steps, and at the top yet another man was waiting for me. He dragged me into a room which reminded me a lot of one at home, with tall sliding doors that separated two large adjoining rooms. In front of the sliding doors there was a small crate of the kind you might sell oranges in. The man barked at me to sit on it and not move under any circumstances.

After two hours an SS man came to fetch me and took me to a room where a friendly looking Dutchman was waiting for me. He started by telling me there was no need to be afraid. This message completely missed the mark: I stood there weak-kneed, my hands trembling with fear. He kindly asked me who had helped me along the way. I shrugged and said I didn't know. I realised that they wanted to know the names of my benefactors. I didn't know anyone's real names, only their made-up ones, and I was very glad of that then. The man tried to persuade me that it would be perfectly all right to say their names and told me in a sugary tone that he wouldn't hurt me, but I just shrugged again. Then he got angry and started shouting, but I didn't understand what he was saying.

The SS man behind me now sprang into action. Although I didn't hear anyone order him to do so, he raised his hand and hit me in the face, very hard. That was the first time in my life I had faced physical violence. When the Germans realised I couldn't answer their questions, they took me back to my little crate by the sliding doors. Half an hour later the door opened and a man whom I recognised appeared. He stood in the doorway, looked at me questioningly and asked how I'd got here. It was Mr Oudshoorn, a policeman from our neighbourhood who was posted to the station on Jonas Daniël Meijerplein. Apparently he was more of a collaborator than we had thought and had ended up in the Sicherheitsdienst (SD), the Nazi security service. In any case, my family and I had known him all my life, and he knew us too. He came up to me, pointed at my cheek and asked what had happened. I gestured mutely towards the other room; I hardly dared utter a word. He shook his head disapprovingly. Then he gave me a wet handkerchief to hold against my swollen cheek and asked, 'Have you ever smoked?'

I had, a few times, very secretly, but I shook my head. He took a packet of cigarettes from his pocket and that afternoon I openly smoked a cigarette for the first time. To this day, I don't know if Mr Oudshoorn had something more in mind with this cigarette, but I rather think he didn't know what else to do. He asked how I had landed in this situation and I told him in telegraphic style what had happened over the last twenty-four hours.

He left the room and returned shortly after. 'Do you know a Mr De Groot on Sint Antoniesbreestraat?' I shook my head again. The man in question was apparently a wholesaler selling perfume on the corner of Sint Antoniesbreestraat and Snoekjessteeg. It all meant nothing to me. 'He saw you get off the tram on Jan Evertsenstraat and reported you to the SD.' As I understand it, reporting a Jew at the time got you a rijksdaalder, or two and a half guilders. That was all Mr Oudshoorn could do for me, and the information was of precious little help.

It was almost evening by this point and I was still sitting on my crate. Suddenly I realised I desperately needed the loo. I asked the next person who came into the room if I could use the toilet, but he didn't respond and left me sitting there. Luckily Mr Oudshoorn came back soon after, and he took me out to the corridor straight away. While I was on the toilet I heard someone tell him to watch out because I'd escaped before. Once I was back on my crate he asked me if that was true, and how I had managed it. I didn't tell him, of course. A little while later the door opened and two SS men came in. One of them told me to get up, and the other stayed in the doorway. It seemed I had to leave and that they were going to take me somewhere else. Another SD man was waiting for me by the staircase; he took me firmly by the arm. At the bottom of the stairs yet another two men were standing ready. They took me away as if I were the worst criminal in the world. Even at the door of the police van there was another one standing guard. People stopped in the street to look at what was happening. I felt an enormous sense of shame being carted off like a thief in full view of these people.

They took me to Euterpestraat (now called Gerrit van der Veenstraat). Not that they told me, as just hearing the name would have made me wet myself. Euterpestraat was the most terrifying image we had in our minds at that time. Countless people had been dragged there and tortured – not just Jews, but also non-Jews were mangled and broken here. And now it was my turn.

Inside, one of my guards asked a question to the soldier stationed at the door, who looked from the man to me with an expression that seemed to say: what on earth is a child doing here?

They took me to the first floor and locked me up in a little room. I must have sat there for about three-quarters of an hour before they came to get me and took me to a German in civilian clothes across from the stairs. They called him Herr Henschel, a name I will never forget. He was very friendly to begin with as well. Although I didn't understand German and certainly didn't speak it, he still expected me to answer. The only thing I could do was shrug. I think he wanted to know how I had managed to get away, but I wasn't sure, and he wouldn't have understood my Dutch in any case. He got terribly angry nevertheless and banged the table with his fist. The SS man beside me kept hold of my shoulder. I was terrified, of course, but I kept my cool. They already had me where they wanted me, after all.

Herr Henschel kept shouting and I had no idea what he was on about. Suddenly he got up and came towards me. I don't know if he ordered the SS man to do it or if he did it of his own accord, but I saw a large hand descending on me. I should have kept still, because when I tried to turn my face away, four fingers landed in my right eye. I felt the right side of my face swell up; tears were dripping down my jaw. A moment later I realised they weren't tears, but blood. All I could do was hope I'd get away with just a bleeding eye.

Once it was over they took me back to the little room, but I didn't have to wait long before two SS men came to fetch me. They took me downstairs and into the street. I was completely at a loss. We crossed the street towards a school. Once inside, they led me to a door that reminded me strongly of my old school, which also had a door like that, one with a brass-coloured bar on it. They opened the door and I found myself looking into a sports hall full of people. Behind the door was a small platform from which three steps led down into the hall. The murderers Ferdinand aus der Fünten and Willy Lages, who co-ordinated the deportation of Dutch Jews, were standing on the platform. They were dead drunk, as usual. Just as I was about to go down, someone kicked me in the back and I fell into the hall without touching the steps. For a moment I lay there, not because I was in pain, but because I wasn't sure what the next attack would be. Someone in the hall tried to help me up, but a voice snarled at him that he should leave off. I got up and joined the crowd, that had clearly been brought here to be deported. Two women tried to tend to my eye because it wouldn't stop bleeding. I did my best to convince them that it was nothing, but they kept on dabbing at it with a wet cloth.

We sat there all night; the following morning we were finally taken in lorries to the Hollandsche Schouwburg. Everybody was very interested in me; it rarely or never happened that a child was brought in alone, of course, so everyone wanted to know all the ins and outs. Not until I was in the lorry did I look round for any familiar faces, but I didn't recognise anyone. I saw a young woman eating a sandwich and suddenly realised I was starving. She noticed and gave me a piece.

We were unloaded on Plantage Middenlaan and lined up. So I'd ended up back at the Hollandsche Schouwburg, but with one difference: this time I was thinking seriously about fleeing, because I'd learned that I knew how to survive. It occurred to me that I'd been very lucky for quite a long time. Of course my luck had run out the day before yesterday, but if I hadn't been given away in Ommen, I might have been able to live there until the end of the war. I would have to wait for a dose of luck, but I needed a large one.

There had probably been a change of guards since I was last here, because nobody treated me like an escapee who should have been put on a transport long ago.

There were a few familiar faces inside the theatre, but everybody was so preoccupied with themselves that no one paid any attention to me. I was given a drink and had to sew a star on to my coat, but I couldn't manage it so they gave me a couple of safety pins so I could fasten on the hated bit of cloth. After that I counted my money; there wasn't much left.

In the hallway was a kind of improvised little shop. It had precious few items for sale, only the most urgent necessities,

The Hollandsche Schouwburg during the war years. (Beeldbank
WO2/NIOD)

like a first aid kit. I enquired if children were allowed to go across the road to sleep and that still seemed to be the case. I bumped into my old teacher again, Mr Hamburg, and he told me that the children had to line up in the hall at five o'clock ready to go to the crèche. I spent the rest of the day wandering aimlessly through the building; it was just as well I was used to spending whole days on my own by now.

The next time I passed by the little shop I looked to see if there was anything there I fancied. There was a whole row of fizzy drink bottles, and I bought one, and then my eye fell on a small tube of sleeping tablets. I still remember the brand name: Sonneril. I had learned not to question why I did things and the tube vanished into my pocket without my paying for it. I'd got pretty good at that from living on the street. I knew one thing for certain: tonight I absolutely had to sleep. The Krauts had already kept me awake for two nights and I wouldn't be able to sleep here in the theatre either – it was far too hectic for that.

Towards five o'clock I made my way to the hall because I wanted to be sure of a mattress in the crèche. I had succeeded in getting there last time, so it was worth another try. Parents and children were coming from all directions. There were SS men around too, of course. As the hall was filling up, Mr Hamburg appeared. He was now wearing an armband. He saw me standing there, came up to me and, taking me by the hand, gently led me in amongst the children and put me in the queue. An SS man watched him do it.

We set off across the road, accompanied on either side by SS soldiers who looked somewhat bored, but made sure there were always enough of them to keep a keen eye on the queue. Once inside, we each got a sandwich and something to drink. Yet again the SS men were in a hurry; on all sides you heard *schnell, schnell*. Not much later we were on our mattresses, under horse blankets; I had already taken my pink sleeping tablet. I had no idea what I was doing, my childish brain thought: swallow and sleep – but of course that didn't happen. After five minutes I still hadn't fallen asleep, so I took a second tablet. Then everything went blank.

In the middle of the night I felt myself being shaken and tugged, and with a superhuman effort I managed to open one eye a tiny fraction. I saw a nurse and a few men. There was an SS man as well, but he was standing right at the back. Someone made a strange remark, something about a swinging fever.

The next morning I half-woke up to find a nurse bending over me and holding my wrist in her hand. I looked at her blankly. She took me to a little room, telling me she had to because the Germans were afraid I had an infectious disease. I fell asleep again, and a few hours later I was taken across the road to a large attic room where a doctor had set up his office. He was going to examine me, while a soldier kept watch at the door. I didn't understand it at all; I didn't feel ill in the least. I tried to say there was nothing wrong with me but it was like talking to a wall. The doctor inspected my throat and then checked my eyes and ears. That must have been quite something, as my ears hadn't been cleaned once since my mother had gone! Next I had to undress, and as I draped my trousers over the chair, the tube of sleeping pills rolled out of my pocket. The soldier picked it up and handed it to the doctor, who read the label. He said something to the soldier and then gave me a few blows that I will remember all my life. They didn't even let me get dressed; instead the soldier dragged me down the stairs half-naked. At the bottom, some people from the Jewish Council quickly got me away from him and took me out of his sight.

★ ★ ★

I only understood much later what all this meant. At the time I couldn't work out what that tube had to do with anything. I didn't know what effect two of those little pills would have on a boy of 13 who had never taken a drug like that before, so I was at a loss as to why the doctor and the soldier were so angry. It never occurred to me for a moment that they had thought I was feigning illness to avoid being deported.

★ ★ ★

I had to keep a low profile that whole day. One of the ladies told me I was lucky there was no transport that day, as they would have put me straight on it. In the late afternoon I went to the hall and just joined the queue, as if nothing had happened. No one took any notice of me. There were different soldiers now in any case. The man who had hauled me down the stairs that morning wasn't one of them; apparently he was on leave.

★ ★ ★

I was entirely focused on surviving; I didn't try to be a hero. Trying to be a hero was what I used to do when I was playing

*in the street. I once dived off the Blauwbrug into the Amstel
for half a stuiver – two and a half cents – but that was something else. Here everything you did was driven by fear.*

★ ★ ★

The doors opened and the procession moved off as usual.
There were fewer Germans around than normal and they
were chatting amongst themselves. When I was nearly
across the road, level with a telephone box and a large
advertising column for VAMI dairy products, the German
next to me turned round and walked to the back of the line
to guide the next children. As if in a trance, I broke off to
the right, heading for Plantage Kerklaan, then turned the
corner towards the entrance of Artis, the Amsterdam zoo.
I expected to feel a hand on my neck at any moment, but
nothing of the sort happened. Then I tore the star from my
coat, crumpled it up and stuck it in my pocket.

A number seven tram was waiting by the zoo entrance,
which was its final stop at the time. I got on and sat down.
I was still waiting for a hand to grab me, so I didn't even
notice when the tram started moving. The guard gave me a
child's ticket and I paid the fare. Seven cents.

All through the trip I sat there stunned. I had escaped
again. At the final stop the guard shook my shoulder and
told me I had to get off, as the tram didn't go any further. Only then did I return to the real world. Back on
the street I looked round carefully; in the first instance I
didn't know where I was. After walking for a while I came
to Jan Evertsenstraat, but that wasn't where I wanted to
be at all – that place was still too fresh in my memory. I

took the very next tram back and got off in the centre of town.

It was already late and I had to find a place to sleep so I made my way as usual towards Nieuwmarkt, to my own familiar surroundings. I knew my way around there. I headed straight for the air raid shelter and collapsed in a corner. And suddenly the tears came. I couldn't hold them back and was crying so uncontrollably that I was afraid people could hear me in the street up above. But at some point I must have fallen asleep.

11

The next morning I woke up early and just sat staring in front of me for a while. I wondered if it had been a dream or if it had all actually happened. But when I felt the pain in my arm and shoulder I knew I hadn't dreamed it. That damned Kraut had really knocked me about! I rubbed my arm and listened to the early fish carts rattling over the cobbles above my head as they went to take their place on Nieuwmarkt.

A little later I crawled out of my hole. First I went to the pump to freshen up my face a bit, as further opportunities to wash were not likely to be forthcoming any time soon. I filled my stomach with water because I had learned that you could ease your hunger a little that way, even if only for a short while. I started my morning walk on Zeedijk and went along Achterburgwal back to Monnikenstraat. There I found a small printing works with its doors wide open. I stopped at the entrance to look at the press rolling. I loved the smell of the ink and breathed it in deeply. Then I saw the man operating the machine give me a strange look and I suppressed the urge to hurry away. Don't rouse suspicion, I thought, never rouse suspicion. Then the man beckoned me, indicating that I was welcome to watch from up close. I didn't dare refuse and went inside but immediately felt suspicious and fearful, as I always did whenever something out of the ordinary happened. After watching for a bit I took off again. The man meant well and had no bad intentions, of course, but my mistrust was growing all the time.

Out of the corner of my eye I had noticed that the front door leading to the apartments above the printing works was open. I looked inside as I went past but couldn't see anyone going in or out. When I walked by again that evening the door was still open. On a whim, I decided to go in and climbed the stairs to the attic. Then I must have fallen asleep because I didn't wake up until early the next morning.

At first I had absolutely no idea where I was. At the tolling of a bell I recognised the sound of the Zuiderkerk tower; it was seven o'clock. Very cautiously I went downstairs but didn't see or hear anyone. I was starving; it was high time to go out on the prowl for food again.

That night I made use of my new sleeping place for a second time. I was beginning to like it there, and it was certainly a much better and especially much cleaner billet than the air raid shelter.

All went well for a few days until one evening I made a fatal error. I headed up to the attic as usual, but for some reason miscounted the staircases and settled down on the third floor landing instead of the fourth, which mostly went unused. I was completely oblivious and fell asleep. Much later that evening – it must still have been before midnight because that's when everyone had to be off the streets – I was woken up. I found myself looking drowsily at four boys who were staring at me as if I were from another planet. The oldest one asked who I was, where I came from and above all how I'd found my way there. As usual I lied from start to finish. He decided I should just join them indoors.

I followed them into a spotless living room in a neat and tidy apartment. We all sat down around the table and then the oldest, who was called Joop, started asking me lots of questions. After a while I realised that he didn't believe a word of what I was telling him and had clearly got me all figured out. While we were talking, two boys came into the room carrying a large quantity of food. They set everything out on the table and everyone started eating. I watched until one of the boys said I should tuck in before all the food disappeared from under my nose. I didn't need to be told twice and almost literally threw myself at the food. I was still stuffing myself long after they'd all finished, but when I realised they were sitting there looking at me, I promptly stopped in embarrassment. Then one of the boys said something remarkable: 'Don't you worry, just go on eating, we'll have fresh stuff all over again tomorrow.' Even a child would have known that wasn't normal in those days, but I happily accepted their hospitality all the same. Once everything had been tidied away I was given a bed in a small room. Belly stuffed, I dropped onto it and instantly fell asleep.

At nine o'clock the next morning I walked into the living room, sleepy-faced; only Joop was still around. When he saw me he went to the kitchen and returned with three sandwiches on a plate. I laughed inwardly. Where on earth had I ended up, seventh heaven? While I ate, Joop picked up one of my shoes and asked me how long I'd been roaming the streets. The holes in my shoes, and the matching ones in my socks, told their own story. He looked at me with an expression of amusement and then started talking calmly. For my own safety I had to keep to a few strict rules: I had to stay indoors all day and do as I was told. Then I could stay. I was only too happy to comply.

Joop had to go out to do some shopping but told me he would be back in the early afternoon. 'If the bell rings, don't open the door, and whatever you do, keep away from the window.' As if I hadn't learned all that long ago.

After Joop left I went on the prowl again after all, but this time in the cupboards. There was food in abundance and I tucked into everything. I didn't feel guilty; that feeling had disappeared over the last few months. In the afternoon Joop came home again with a bag full of food and by six o'clock all the boys were back.

After supper they started whispering a bit and I pricked up my ears. From what I could hear, I understood that 'the takings from the next action' were for me, but I had no idea what they meant by that. Later, when they spoke about it a bit more openly, I learned that these boys kept an eye out for places where Jews were being taken away. If the people in question had a shop or another kind of business, they broke in at night and took valuable goods from the premises, things like weighing scales and cash registers. That's what they lived off. Only they had to be quick, or else Puls would beat them to it.

★ ★ ★

Puls was a removal firm hired by the Germans to clear Jewish houses and businesses whose owners had been taken away on transport. The goods were stored in warehouses and there the valuable items were subsequently picked out. It's well known that Göring and Goebbels acquired many antiques and works of art in this way.

★ ★ ★

The boys had a lot of fun that evening. They told each other jokes that went completely over my head. What I did understand was that I had become one of them, and that's how they treated me too.

In the morning I was woken up by all the noise the boys were making. I got up, washed, dressed and joined them for breakfast. I could tell from their exuberance that Joop wasn't around, but I didn't dare ask where he was. Joop was my only support just then. I was still eating when he came in holding a parcel wrapped in brown paper. When he

The Dutch Nazi party's removal firm, A. Puls. (Beeldbank WO2/ NIOD)

removed the paper a pair of black ankle boots appeared. He placed them on the table, right in front of my nose. I sat and stared at them speechlessly. The boys examined the shoes in great detail and they all found something to say about them. You could see from their faces that they were happy for me. One of them asked Joop how much he'd had to pay.

'Thirty-five guilders,' Joop said with great indignation. 'Nothing but thieves on the black market.'

I burst out laughing, because of course he'd paid with money that he hadn't exactly come by in an honest way either, but that didn't worry me. Better they got it than those thieves at Puls.

That day a lot of other things happened as well. Joop took me outside, to Uilenburgerstraat, because there was a bathhouse there; given my condition, a good scrubbing wasn't exactly an indulgence. I was given a piece of substitute soap, which didn't make a lather, but even so a great sense of well-being poured over me along with the water. When the bath attendant called, 'High time!', I dried myself off and got dressed again.

All that time Joop sat patiently waiting for me. I had a brand new friend.

From Uilenburgerstraat we went down Batavierstraat and Oudeschans to Rechtboomssloot, to my new *chaver*'s barber. When I sat down in the chair, the man looked first at my extremely long hair and then at Joop, who grinned sheepishly before looking away.

We walked via Nieuwmarkt and Lange Niezel to Damrak, where we made a beeline for C&A to buy me some clothes. Joop walked up to a sales-lady and spoke to her briefly. In no time at all a miracle unfolded before my very eyes: a new pair of trousers, a new blazer. Once everything was to Joop's satisfaction, the lady brought out a rayon shirt and, as the icing on the cake, my very first tie. It truly was a glorious moment.

Joop and the sales-lady went to the checkout to pay. Apart from money he also had a stack of clothing coupons, as you couldn't buy anything at all without those. He'd got them from the black market too, no doubt; you could get absolutely anything there if you had the cash. From the discussion that followed I understood that he didn't have enough coupons and therefore couldn't buy all the clothes. After a little back and forth, the sales-lady suggested that she would go and talk it over with her boss, but my generous friend didn't like that idea. I thought I saw some money furtively change hands, and then the deal was done. The sales-lady helped me into my blazer and took me to the mirror. Joop unwrapped the shoes from their paper packaging and there I stood with all my new acquisitions. Looking in the mirror I didn't know whether to laugh or cry, and all the while Joop stood watching me with a certain pride.

Walking along the street I glanced at myself in all the shop windows. We were heading towards Central Station but we didn't get that far because, when we passed the Cineac cinema, Joop asked if I'd like to go in. The show was a continuous reel of mostly news followed by a cartoon, the whole thing lasting exactly fifty-five minutes. The news was mainly about the victorious glory of the German army, nothing but propaganda for the war. When someone came round with a collection box, Joop gave a cent to the Winter Relief, the National Socialist organisation that collected money in line with the Nazi philosophy that there should be no poverty or need among the people. Not donating would have looked suspicious. He glanced at me and grinned a bit.

To crown this festive day he took me to a real restaurant at the bottom of Damrak called De Bock. I felt like a king! The plate was divided into sections: one for potatoes, one for spinach, and in the third was an egg with a knob of butter. Joop had to hand over an extra coupon for the butter.

★ ★ ★

This happened almost seventy years ago, but I'll remember that feast my whole life. I'll never forget Joop either. I would so love to meet those boys again, as well as all the other people who saved my life, or who at least tried to make it more pleasant.

★ ★ ★

When we returned to Monnikenstraat late in the afternoon, I was greeted with a chorus of oohs and aahs. They all sat gaping at me and tried to make me feel as bashful as possible, with complete success. Once I was in bed the first tears came, but this time they were tears of joy. I hadn't shed those for a very long time.

One evening, after I'd been with them for about five days, Joop and I came in to find an object on the table covered with a cloth. One of the boys went and stood next to the cloth like a ringmaster, made his hand into a trumpet and blew a fanfare. Then he whisked the cloth away and to my surprise there was a hutch with a rabbit inside. A gift for me. They'd probably found the animal in a home where the people had been taken away and brought it with them because it would have died otherwise. The boys couldn't have made me happier. How could I have moved from hell to heaven so quickly?

The hutch went straight into my little room, but of course that meant I had to go out the next day to find vegetable scraps. I walked the streets as if nothing could happen to me, and as long as I didn't meet anyone I knew, there was basically nothing to worry about. I wasn't really conscious of danger any more because I could calmly bide my time in Amsterdam like this until the end of the war. There were still raids now and then but that was no longer my affair, I just went home to Monnikenstraat.

Because I looked decent again, my self-esteem and confidence returned. Nobody noticed a blond, blue-eyed boy who looked perfectly acceptable, and I was far too young to be sent to Germany as a labourer. Besides, I was always with my friends, who took good care of me.

And so I once again made the mistake of hoping I could stay put until the end of the war, and once again my sleep was disturbed most unpleasantly.

It must have been around two o'clock in the morning when a complete stranger woke me up and demanded that I get up and come to the living room. When I got there I saw all my friends sitting in a row on the floor with their backs against the wall. I joined them.

One of the two men went downstairs and the other told us that we'd all be sent to an institution for juvenile delinquents. For the boys it was a disaster, but for me it was a solution handed down from heaven. Nobody suspected I was Jewish; I was just one of the burglars, and so I was off to the institution. Where could I be safer or better off than there? Together with my friends, at that!

After we'd waited a long time the first man came back upstairs to inform us that the police van was ready to leave. The boys were sent downstairs one by one. I was up last, but when my turn came, the man who had woken me up told me I didn't belong with those boys. He went on for a while without me understanding much of what he was talking about, but the gist was that I had to make myself scarce at six o'clock sharp, when the curfew ended. He would come back later to check if I had done as he said, and if I hadn't, I would join the others after all.

I sat waiting for him until nine, but to my great regret he didn't return. After a substantial breakfast I just went out onto the streets. I'd become so brazen that I even stayed a few more nights in the place, but when the food was all gone I stopped risking it and moved back to the air raid shelter. My fear of sleeping on my own in the apartment became too much. I tried not to think about what became of my rabbit. After just over a week in the apartment, I had to carry on again on my own.

12

It was very strange, but every time I had to fall back on the air raid shelter or some other dark place, I came out stronger. I still think about that period an awful lot – not because it was so terrible or because I felt so sorry for myself, but because I hardly spared a thought for my father, mother or brothers back then. If someone had predicted what was in store for me, I would have told them that I couldn't possibly survive it without my parents. I would never have believed that whole days would go by without me thinking of them.

★ ★ ★

I slept by turns in the shelter and in stairwells. I preferred the latter because my new clothes didn't get so dirty there.

My wanderings took me to Waterlooplein for a change, because however nice my clothes were, I was hungry. Thanks to my recent regular meals, and especially the size of them, my stomach now needed more than in the times when I'd had nothing to eat. Later I heard that even the people in the camps, who rarely or never got anything to eat, to some extent got used to it, although you never really get used to that sort of misery, of course.

But pilfering food went much worse for me on Waterlooplein. I still knew many stall owners from when we, my family, used to go shopping there. One man behind a fruit stall recognised me and called me over. I hesitated. He might have been a collaborator – that was always possible, of course. When he gave me a reassuring look I went up to him after all. Straight away he asked after my father. I didn't reply but that said enough. He gave me an apple which I devoured straight away, and far too greedily at that. He gave me another one which vanished just as quickly. Then he took me behind the stall and asked, 'When did you last eat?'

I looked at him and didn't reply. I wasn't too keen on the whole business. Then, out of the blue, he told me to come to Kloveniersburgwal at six o'clock.

I went there just before six but didn't ring the bell. I just watched the house from across the water; I was suspicious and wasn't about to go to any old address that a complete stranger cared to give me. I felt I was worth more than a rijksdaalder.

I didn't know what else to do so I stood and watched for a while. After about twenty minutes I saw a man go in. I was glad then that I hadn't rung the bell. Every stranger was an enemy until proven otherwise. Even as an adult it was hard to judge people back then, let alone as a child. After about half an hour the man came out again and went back the way he had come. Then I left and went back to my bolthole in the air raid shelter that night.

Now that I was on my own again, I realised I had built up a certain routine which had been interrupted by my stay with my friends on Monnikenstraat. So it came about that I had to go to the loo urgently, but discovered there was no newspaper left in the corner of the shelter. Before my time on Monnikenstraat, that had been part of my routine:

whenever I happened upon a newspaper somewhere, I diligently picked it up and took it with me. That's how quickly people get used to luxuries: within a week I'd found it completely natural for everything to just be provided. Especially under Joop's care.

I then asked myself for the first time what might have happened to the boys, as they had entirely vanished from my thoughts too. I wondered if they still thought of me sometimes.

The next morning at eight o'clock there was another raid. They were no longer as big as they had been in the previous months – nearly all the people had been deported by now – but barriers still went up all over the place and you saw people being taken away again. I walked right through the middle of this raid on my way to Waterlooplein and I wasn't even scared; it certainly didn't cross my mind to run away. New clothes, no star – they didn't want me and no one bothered me. It may have been perilous, but I didn't feel any fear at that moment; in fact, I didn't feel anything at all, not even pity for the people being taken away.

I no longer understood myself. That wasn't how I'd been brought up, was it? But all I could think of was self-preservation.

I walked through the market and passed the man who had invited me to Kloveniersburgwal the previous day. When he saw me, he beckoned me over.

'Better come behind the stall,' he said, 'so people will think you are with me.'

Then I understood that he knew exactly what my situation was. That was dangerous – but if he meant me any harm, he would have reported me by now. I did as he asked and went behind the stall.

'Have you eaten yet?' he asked.

I shook my head, and he opened a box and produced a little tin. When he opened it there were a couple of delicious sandwiches grinning up at me.

'Go ahead,' he said.

I certainly didn't need telling twice. After that he let me choose some fruit. Without me noticing it, the raid had ended. Then the man began talking to me very seriously, asking why I hadn't come to his house yesterday. I looked at him, feeling a bit shy, and told him that I'd been at his front door, but that I hadn't dared to knock in the end. When he said he didn't believe me, I told him I'd seen a man call at his house and then leave again a little later.

He gave me a look and started laughing. 'No need to worry about you!' he said. Then he stopped and said gravely, 'The man you saw yesterday came for you. He might have had an address where you could go into hiding. That's why I asked him to come.'

I stayed with the fruit-seller all day; I never learned his name. In the evening he took me home with him and we had dinner with his wife, but afterwards I had to leave because they had to go out somewhere. We arranged that I would come to his stall the next day at four o'clock instead of hanging around there all day, because that was bound to attract attention and people might wonder what I was doing there.

That night I slept very restlessly. It was as if tomorrow was my birthday and I didn't know what presents I would get. The day dragged on. I suddenly realised how eager I was to go and see my new friend. That's what he was to me. At four o'clock I went to his stall and he told me to go ahead to his house and wait for him there. His wife knew I was coming.

I headed towards Kloveniersburgwal but I wasn't in a great hurry to get there. I felt uneasy again, but the prospect of getting food pushed aside all my concerns. When I rang the bell, the door opened almost immediately and the woman greeted me very warmly. It made me feel terribly shy. After I'd timidly looked round a bit, she sat me down in a large armchair and took a seat opposite me. She knew I was Jewish but it didn't seem to bother her much.

After a while she got up and fetched a teapot and two cups, and after pouring the tea, she went to the cupboard and returned with two small plates piled with delicious sweets. My mouth started to water. I'd had plenty to eat over the last few weeks, but it had been a very long time since I'd eaten such rare treats as these. The woman saw me looking at all those goodies and told me that this was the perk that came with having food to trade: you could swap fruit and vegetables for cake. She preferred cake to fruit, she added with a chuckle.

I took a sip of tea, though it didn't interest me in the least. But I didn't dare to start on the cakes before she did. Sadly they all disappeared much quicker than I'd wanted: bite, gulp, gone. Before I'd spent half an hour in that house I found myself getting used to feeling 'at home' again.

★ ★ ★

Every time I found my way to the homes of strangers who made me feel welcome, I was like a puppy. You just had to give me a pat on the head and a nice bone and I instantly had a new home, although I subconsciously knew very well that it was probably temporary. The people I came into contact with were for the most part very kind because of that animal instinct in me. People with neshama, with soul, who were willing to help.

You didn't see the other kind of people, and if they saw you, they looked right through you. Once I was lucky enough to find a coupon for a bread roll, but I was three cents short of the amount needed. Then I met a family acquaintance and told him how I'd found the coupon, but that I needed another three cents to be able to actually buy the roll. 'That's too bad,' he said and walked off.

★ ★ ★

At about six o'clock the man came home from the market and greeted his wife with a kiss. That touched me so deeply that tears welled up in my eyes. I hadn't seen any little gestures like that for so long; I could hardly remember how families behaved, let alone that little intimacies like that played a role.

My host then sat down and took a long look at me. I quite understood that it must have seemed very strange that a young boy could live on the street alone, without his parents, and yet hold his own. Of course, I also understood that he was curious about how I'd managed it, especially as I'd never had to live like that before. He started to ask me frank questions and I tried to answer as honestly as possible, but while I was telling my story, things came up that I could barely remember even though they had only happened a month ago. It seemed that I simply forgot the nasty bits as soon as I could. Maybe that's hard to imagine nowadays, but back then it was as if you forgot things on purpose, or at least didn't want to talk about them and therefore kept them quiet.

After a while my answers started to get less and less coherent because I could hear more interesting sounds coming from the kitchen. My full attention was focused on the bowls that were being brought in. The man soon noticed and stopped asking questions.

The meal I was served was truly fit for a king. Really, it was all there. Soup, potatoes, vegetables, meat and gravy – there was no end to it. I suppose I'd eaten well with the boys on Monnikenstraat, but this was a whole new level. I was unstoppable and they just let me get on with it. I didn't even feel I had to mind my manners and say that I'd had enough before I was full, nor did I feel the need to restrain myself. For a short time I truly felt completely at ease, and only in hindsight did I realise that these two good people had loved watching me. To cap it all, there was pudding! I can't bear to think of it now, but I believe I devoured half of it.

We'd only just finished eating when the bell rang and the man I'd seen the day before came in. He was a gruff fellow and not exactly friendly at first glance; that was something I'd become very sensitive to. The two men sat and talked and then, both in turn, gave the woman a meaningful look, upon which she got up to clear the table and asked me to help. I didn't realise that whatever the men were discussing at that moment was not meant for my ears.

After a while my host called us back in and asked me to take a seat. They told me bluntly that if I were to leave, I wouldn't be allowed to come back. That gave me such a shock that the woman immediately put her arms around me, wanting to console me, but then the gruff man explained everything. He told me that it would be far too dangerous for me (and for them too, of course). He immediately added that it didn't mean I had to go back to the shelter; I would be all right from now on as long as I did exactly as I was told.

I was going to live at his house for a few days; he wouldn't be around much himself. He lived on Raamgracht, not far from where we were just then, and he was going to take me there shortly.

'Once you're inside, you mustn't go out in the street any more. But there are plenty of books and lots of food too, so you won't be bored,' he said. 'I'll come by with more food from time to time.'

When it began to get dark, I said goodbye to my new friends and went away with the man, whose name was Bertus. Once we arrived at the house on Raamgracht, he showed me around. There was a large double bed for me to sleep in. After explaining everything he said he had to go out again for a while, but that I was welcome to go to bed and didn't have to wait up for him.

As soon as I was on my own, I started exploring. The first thing I did was to look for a rear exit, as my instinct for self-preservation drove me to make a list of escape routes before anything else. Once I'd done my rounds, I realised that there was only one bed in the house. I didn't like that; the thought of sleeping in the same bed as Bertus didn't appeal to me much. I hadn't liked sharing a bed with Uncle Joop either when I'd stayed with him. All the same, I got undressed and lay down, the second luxurious experience of the day: first that meal, and now a real bed too. I fell asleep straight away.

When I woke up the next morning I was alone, and that seemed to have been the case all night because the other side of the bed was still neatly made and the pillow was smooth. I got up and took the opportunity to wash thoroughly; you never knew when the next one would come. Being occupied in this way, I didn't hear Bertus come in and turned to find him watching me.

'So,' he said, 'they taught you that well at home.' Then he held up a large sack. 'A present for you, from your friend,' he explained.

I hastily dried myself and threw on my clothes. I found it rather embarrassing that the man had seen me naked. When I came back into the room and looked inside the sack, I saw lots of fruit. You can't imagine how I felt just then. Bertus sat for a while without saying anything. I was silent too; I didn't even ask why he hadn't been home that night, because I wasn't really interested. I just went along with everything.

Bertus then told me we would be off together soon, but he didn't say where. However, he did impress upon me to stay indoors and above all not to open the door, even if the bell rang. He also mentioned that it would be for the best if I stayed away from the windows, of course. After a good half hour he left, saying that he wasn't sure exactly when he would be back. I didn't mind as I wasn't bored in the least.

At four o'clock Bertus returned and said he would cook dinner. Because I didn't have anything better to do, I helped him as much as I was able. Bertus seemed awfully good at it, but it struck me that there was no woman around, even though there were many signs that a woman had been there at some point: a kitchen table with two chairs, and other little details suggesting the presence of a second person.

When dinner was ready we sat down to eat, facing each other across the table. I finished first, upon which he gave me a kindly look for the first time and told me to go ahead and finish what was left in the pans, as he was already full. Afterwards he asked if I would do the washing up, as he had to pop out again.

Just before he left, he called back to me that I should go to bed and not wait up for him. I was so used to being alone that it didn't even occur to me to wait. Once I'd done the dishes and it had got dark, I went to bed.

The next morning it was once again clear that I'd been the only one sleeping in the bed. I did think it was a bit odd, but it still didn't really bother me.

Bertus didn't show up again until late on Saturday afternoon. It felt good to have him around again; I was living in a state of some uncertainty and I was really very dependent on him. Before he sat down, he made a pot of tea and called me over to the kitchen. As he poured the tea, he said in a reassuring voice, 'Tomorrow morning we're going away; this is your last day here. I'm sorry that you have to stay indoors all the time, but that'll soon be over. First we have to get you safely out of Amsterdam.'

I asked where we were going and he replied that he couldn't tell me, for safety reasons. I accepted that. After finishing his tea he went for a quick lie down on the bed because he hadn't slept very much the previous night. Before I knew it, I heard him snoring loudly. I hardly dared move for fear of waking him up.

That evening we had sandwiches, and at about nine o'clock he had to pop out again. I spent yet another night alone, but now that I knew how loud he snored, I wasn't sorry.

★ ★ ★

Only much later did I realise that the house probably didn't belong to him at all. No doubt the inhabitants had been taken away, and the house was used by me, and probably also by many others, as a safe haven until he found me a hiding place.

13

The next morning he arrived early. We were both a little nervous. This time I closed the kitchen door while washing, and he must have got the message loud and clear because he didn't come in.

After I got dressed we had a sandwich, and once we'd tidied everything away and cleaned up, he took a last look round and said we'd better go. My heart started thumping; for the umpteenth time I was dependent on other people and had no idea what was going to happen to me. Outside the sun was already high in the sky and it was getting pretty warm. I hadn't been outdoors for some time, and the old, slightly stuffy canal-side house didn't get any sun, so I hadn't noticed the beautiful weather.

We set off towards the city centre, but I didn't dare ask any questions. We came to a tram stop and boarded a tram. It was a lovely ride and I savoured the fresh air to the full. We got off by a large square that I'd never visited before. It turned out that this was Haarlemmermeer station, our apparent point of departure. I hadn't even known it existed. In front of the station there were German soldiers.

'If they stop us,' Bertus said out of the blue, 'I'll just keep walking, because you'll be done for in any case.'

That was just about the worst thing he could have said to me at such a critical moment, and a feeling of panic gripped me by the throat. With the courage of desperation I stayed by his side and kept walking towards the soldiers.

We entered the station rigid with fear, but no one took any notice of us. Bertus bought two tickets – where to, I had no idea. There were soldiers walking around on the platform too. We boarded a train which stood ready to depart and nothing at all happened; no one bothered us.

I don't remember how long the journey took but it felt like an eternity. How could Bertus have made such a tactless remark? He'd made everything much worse, and as calm as I had been of late in these sorts of situations, I was all the more nervous now.

We got off at a station in a little village, and to our relief there was not a soldier to be seen. We were also the only people getting off the train. On the board above the only bench on the platform I read 'De Kwakel'.

We left the little station and came to an old village situated on a long road with a canal on either side. You could only reach the houses by crossing a gangway or a little bridge over the water. The gangways leading to some of the houses had been drawn parallel to the bank, so you had to pull them towards you with a hook before you could cross. Luckily the house we were apparently aiming for had a fixed gangplank.

We were obviously expected because the door opened straight away and a man came out. He first shook Bertus's hand before welcoming me and introducing himself as Mr Voorn. We went into a cosy living room where the lady of the house got up and greeted Bertus like an old acquaintance. She poured some coffee and they chatted about this and that. I sat there a little forlorn; they hardly spoke to me. Of course, it was hard to talk to a child whom you'd never seen before and knew nothing about.

At some point Mrs Voorn fetched a tray from the kitchen and began laying the table. When everything was ready we all sat down. I spotted a bowl of runner beans, which I'd always loathed. After my plate had been piled up high, Mr and Mrs Voorn began to pray. Bertus and I didn't join in. First they crossed themselves, which I had never understood, and then they muttered a prayer so unbelievably quickly that I didn't catch a word. Once it was over we were allowed to tuck in. Mr and Mrs Voorn told me to eat as much as I wanted, and that I didn't need to be embarrassed. That remark touched me.

After the meal – and more prayers – Mr Voorn asked if I would pop over to the neighbours across the way to fetch a saw. The man who lived there would know what I'd come for. So I went over and looked for a bell, but I couldn't see one at all. Luckily there was no need for one, as the door swung open and a man invited me in. He took me into a room where two people were sitting: a man to the left of the window and a woman to the right.

'So,' the man who'd opened the door said to me, 'you've come for the saw.'

I nodded and he asked me to wait while he fetched it from the shed. I stood forlornly in the middle of the room while the man and woman by the window inspected me from head to toe. I began to feel more and more uncomfortable; there was something very unsettling about the whole situation. I wasn't afraid, but I felt there was a very uneasy atmosphere. Then the man came back with the saw. He stood in the doorway, so I could see him as well as the couple by the window.

Then something happened that I'll never forget. The men held each other's gaze for a moment, and then the man at the window gave a barely perceptible nod.

I'd been sold, disposed of. Weighed and declared sound, as if I was an auction lot. I found it very humiliating.

When I returned with the saw I felt like saying to Bertus, 'Please just take me back to my air raid shelter', but my good sense told me not to.

Bertus left that afternoon and I stayed behind, feeling lonely and deeply unhappy after what I felt had been such a miserable incident at the neighbour's house.

★ ★ ★

My situation wasn't so bad, of course, but so much had happened to me by then that my outlook on the world had been warped. The only thing I knew by then was how to survive in an absurd world that I barely recognised and which had been utterly distorted by the war. Later I found out that my experiences weren't too bad at all compared to those of some others. There were plenty of people in hiding who had experienced much harder times, to say nothing of the ones in the camps.

★ ★ ★

That night I slept yet again in a new bed – something I was beginning to get used to. At the start of the war I had always felt uncomfortable in unfamiliar houses, and whenever I lay alone in a strange bed at night I couldn't hold back my tears. But that had stopped happening recently. That night, however, I lay awake for a long time, because I felt as though I'd put my destiny into other people's hands, and that wasn't a pleasant feeling. I had lost my autonomy. In Amsterdam I'd made up my own mind about what I was or wasn't going to do; here, I had to stand idly by and had no control over anything any more.

★ ★ ★

Since the end of the war, self-determination has become essential for me. Freedom is the most important asset left to me from those years.

★ ★ ★

The next morning I woke up early, around six o'clock. Mr Voorn was a coalman, Mrs Voorn had a very large kitchen garden behind the house, and so they were used to starting work early in the morning. I got up, got dressed and looked for somewhere to have a wash, but there was nothing on the first floor. I went downstairs and shyly asked Mrs Voorn where I could clean myself up. She showed me to the scullery, which had a large trough with a big pump at the end and one of those beautiful copper handles. I swung the handle up and down a few times and a broad stream of water splashed out which I had to make very swift use of.

I went back upstairs to make my bed and then Mrs Voorn gave me a sandwich ahead of breakfast, but I had to wait until everyone came back in before I got any more. At half past eight she laid the table, then went to the back door that opened from the scullery, as she called it, into the garden and shouted something I didn't understand. Four men came in, three of whom I hadn't seen before. They all sat down and started eating while the woman served them coffee from a large iron kettle. I picked up a sandwich that was so huge I could only stare at it to begin with. One of the men saw me looking at it.

'These aren't sandwiches for townies, they're real ones,' he said. 'We still bake our own bread,' he added proudly.

One thing was for sure: I thought it was wonderful. Fifteen minutes later everything was gone and they all went back to work, apart from Mr Voorn. He remained at the table and said to Mrs Voorn, 'They'll be here soon.'

I had no idea who 'they' were, but I didn't like it one bit. I was instantly on my guard, although I did my best not to show it. For me, the only 'they' were the Germans. I got up and stood a bit closer to the door, more or less on the starting blocks.

A little while later I saw two men cycling towards us, heading straight for the house. I recognised one of them as the man who had given the nod yesterday. And then I suddenly understood the whole operation.

The men came in and greeted Mr and Mrs Voorn. Then they turned to me and shook my hand. The man I'd seen the previous day was called Arie and the other one's name was Cor. No one said anything else at first. For safety's sake I stayed on the alert, because I wasn't sure if these two men were the aforementioned 'they'.

After coffee, Arie said we'd have to be off because they wanted to be back home before lunch. It wasn't ten o'clock yet, so that meant we had a fair way to go on the bike. That was when it sunk in that I had a hiding place, a permanent address.

★ ★ ★

At that time I still had no clear idea what going into hiding really involved. I think it meant something different for everyone: for one person a godsend, for another an ordeal. It depended entirely on who you ended up with, how they related to you and how they treated you. I had a wonderful time ahead of me, but I didn't know it just then.

★ ★ ★

When we cycled off I was terribly anxious again. The problem was that everything was so sneaky and furtive. I wasn't allowed to know where I was going – that would be far too dangerous, and the safety of the people I was going to was at enough risk as it was. At the same time I had nothing to offer me any certainty at all, but Arie and Cor had no idea of the jumble of thoughts and feelings rushing through me. And how could they have known? They weren't on the run; they had never felt those fears. To them it was obvious that I should resign myself to the situation and put my life into their hands with complete trust.

After a while Arie and Cor swapped bikes, and so I spent the journey sitting behind first one, then the other, on a cushion mounted on a pannier rack, just like how I sometimes used to sit behind my father when we went out by bike. We had been going for at least two hours when we reached the village which was to become my second home. It had such a long name that I couldn't even read it at first. Roelofarendsveen.

★ ★ ★

Only on 23 December 2009 did I learn how exactly it had come about. The man with the saw was married to a close friend of Arie's wife. Purely by chance, they had come that day to visit the neighbours living opposite the Voorns and had learned of my existence. They immediately offered to take me in and give me a safe home. The awful feeling of having been sold has at last been entirely erased, sixty-five years later, because Arie and his wife were the best thing that had happened to me so far.

14

And so, in July 1943, at quarter past twelve, I ended up with a family of three adults: an old, sickly, but ever-so-friendly man, Jan Rekvoort; Arie Verdel, his adopted son; and Arie's wife Mien Hillebrand.

Once I'd introduced myself to everybody we sat down to lunch. At home, before the war, I'd never been a big eater and I fortunately went back to that old habit, giving up eating for eating's sake. I sat next to old Mr Rekvoort. I felt really comfortable around him, although he didn't talk much.

After lunch Mr Rekvoort went up a few steps into a little side room for a nap, the others went back to work, and I stayed behind with Mien. First she showed me the house and what was to be my bedroom. It was a large room, equipped with every convenience. It had a big empty wardrobe where I could put all my stuff. But what stuff? The clothes I was wearing were the only ones I owned! That was soon to change, however.

After the tour Mien and I went to the barn. That was where all the flowers were tended before they went to auction. We climbed the stairs to the loft, where there were a few mattresses and blankets on the floor.

'And this is where the chaps sleep who are in hiding,' said Mien matter-of-factly.

Mien and Arie
Verdel. (Courtesy
of Fiety Lesgever)

Mien & Arie Verdel

I stared at her, dumbstruck.

'Yes,' she said with a shrug, 'otherwise those boys will have
to go to Germany for the *Arbeitseinsatz*. So they sleep here.'
She was referring to the German forced labour programme.

That was Roelofarendsveen for you.

After that we went for a walk between the greenhouses
and across the fields. They covered a large area, and all
sorts of crops were grown there. Some of the land could be
used for horticulture (mostly flowers), but by order of the
Germans a part had to be used for food, including various
kinds of fruit and vegetables.

The Verdels had a medium-sized market-gardening business; part of it bordered on the house, and another part was
further afield.

The following day I was put straight to work, which pleased me enormously. Everything was new and exciting. I'd arrived in melon-picking season. Every day felt like a miracle. There was plenty of food, and I even had a bedroom of my own.

I had become part of a family again overnight. As usual, I settled into my new situation quickly, but the Verdel family also had a knack for adapting to change. Almost from the moment I arrived they saw my presence as the most natural thing in the world, as if it had never been otherwise. Before I knew it, I had been welcomed not only into the family, but also into the village. People I didn't know spoke to me as if they'd known me for years.

That's how I changed in a very short time from a city-boy into a farmer's son. I got to know every aspect of the horticultural trade. I soaked up the new knowledge like a sponge and wanted to master everything as quickly as possible. I learned all I could not only from Arie, but also from other farmers. Our neighbour Jaap de Jong in particular taught me a lot. He showed me how to make the best tobacco.

★ ★ ★

In those days the best tobacco plant was the 'Ingenieur Slietch 25'. When the plant was about five feet tall and the leaves were fully grown, we would pick them and dry them. Then we'd put them in a large tin and bury them in the dung heap for a few weeks. It was always damp and warm in there, so they could ferment undisturbed and acquire their intense aroma. After that the leaves would be dried once more and cut

*up very finely with an old razor blade, and then everyone had
something to smoke again (for a price).*

       ★ ★ ★

In summer the days started at six in the morning and ended
at ten at night. Then we went straight to bed, to be up again
the next day at half past five. I revelled in the fresh air and
the work outdoors.

       ★ ★ ★

*Where I live now, I can smell that same scent every morn-
ing in early spring and in the humid autumn. I say to my
wife, 'I can smell de Veen again.' ('De Veen' is the local
name for Roelofarendsveen.) But then I only live about six
miles away.*

       ★ ★ ★

Working in the polder was the best of all for me. We had to
get there by boat, which I thought was brilliant. No wonder
– as a child of the city, I hadn't done more than sneak a ride
on the back of a horse and cart. I was intensely happy living
with the Verdels, who were a gift that had simply fallen into
my lap, and I adored old Mr Rekvoort.

       ★ ★ ★

*I remember him as a quiet, calm man who kept an eye on
everything. He had his particular habits. For example, I*

always watched closely when he got on his bike. There was a little rod attached to the hub of the back wheel. Everyone else would just put their left foot on the pedal and swing their other leg over the saddle, but he would always stand with his right foot on the rod and swing himself over the bike, an image I will never forget.

★ ★ ★

Arie was lame in one leg. He told me he'd had tuberculosis as a child and spent a few years in bed, so his muscles had never fully developed. Mien's background was quite something. She'd grown up in a family of fifteen. Her father was the village postman and I'd never encountered such an amazing family in all my life; for me, spending time with them was always a celebration. Tragically, one day, when Mien's father was out in a boat on the Braassemermeer with some of his children, he had a heart attack out on the water and died.

Every spare minute I had I spent with Mien's family, which was teeming with kids my own age. I was always struck by how strictly organised the family was; although it was big, it ran like a well-oiled machine. There was a schedule hanging in the kitchen which everyone followed precisely. It listed who was responsible for what, from peeling potatoes to cleaning shoes.

On the farm where I worked, there was a farmhand about my age named Harry van de Wereld. He was my very best friend for the rest of the war, and we got into all kinds of scrapes.

Chapter 14

★ ★ ★

After the war I lost touch with him and only found him again in 1994. Sadly he died a year later.

★ ★ ★

As I mentioned, I wasn't the only person in hiding there, but the others slept in the barn, which didn't seem to worry anyone. I sometimes slept there too. They were all older than me, and they helped work the land in return for being able to hide there. I had a good time with them too, and we were good mates. One afternoon I had coffee in the barn with four of the other farmhands. While chatting to them, I learned that three of them didn't hail from Roelofarendsveen.

'Where are you from then?' I asked one of them.

He didn't answer at first, but looked over at the oldest farmhand, who started laughing and said, 'He's one of your lot too.'

The whole of Roelofarendsveen was full of people in hiding, and it quickly became obvious to everyone that I was a Jewish child, but no one ever mentioned it to me. Nobody cared either. The Veenders (as the people of Roelofarendsveen were called, and still are today) had big hearts.

In September 1944, after about fourteen months with the Verdels, I learned that I had to move because there wasn't enough room for me. It was terrible and I didn't understand it at all, but I didn't ask any questions. I didn't show what I felt. I found it unfair, but they wouldn't explain in any case. That wasn't just because of the war; it was also part of the nature of the people there. I did think it was peculiar, because I knew exactly what went on in the house and I'd never noticed any lack of space. But I resigned myself to the situation, in part because Arie and Mien had already found another address for me. I knew so many people by now that I was sure it couldn't be an insurmountable problem. I was still only a child and Arie and Mien wanted to protect me, so they didn't tell me the real reason why I had to go.

★ ★ ★

On Queen's Day in 1955 I told the story about my years in hiding during an interview on the local radio and this detail happened to come up. Afterwards I received a letter from Mien telling me what the real reason had been. One of the men in hiding who had arrived a bit later turned out to be a deserter from the SS, but because Arie and Mien were still suspicious of him, I had to be taken somewhere safe. This strategy would have made very little difference if the SS man had meant any harm, as my new address was only ten minutes down the road and I had even drunk coffee with him in the barn, where they all slept. But it did clarify matters.

★ ★ ★

On the day of the move my nerves started to play up again. After nearly a year and a half of security, doubt and fear crept back. I was to move down the road from Noordeinde to Zuideinde. Roelofarendsveen and De Kwakel were like two peas in a pod in that respect: both were stretched out on a long road lined with small canals on either side, and houses behind the canals.

My possessions had expanded quite a bit since my arrival, so my luggage was loaded on a wheelbarrow and that's how we arrived at 99 Zuideinde. Mother Mijntje was waiting for us at the door with her hands folded over her belly, and she led us inside. I'd only just entered when father Kees came in from the fields to have his lunch. He was a short man with a cap, which I only ever saw sitting on top of his round head.

'You've got a good nose – lunch is almost ready,' was the first thing he said to me.

Mijntje was a sweet, quiet woman with intelligent eyes which never missed a trick. Everything in the house was sacred to her and she was always the last one to go to bed. They had a daughter, Clara, who was about ten years older than me. Right from the beginning, everyone acted as if I'd been there for years.

No one said much during the meal; only Kees sometimes came out with something. He chatted a bit and suddenly asked me where I was from.

'Amsterdam,' I said.

'Wrong. You come from Rotterdam, you lost your home in the bombing, and now you're living here temporarily. You must never forget that.' A moment later, without even looking up from his plate, he said, 'While I remember, I've got a new bike waiting for you in the barn. You just need to put some air in the tyres.'

I was flabbergasted, but I don't think anyone noticed. This kind of thing apparently came so naturally to these people that it wasn't even worthy of note. And me? I even forgot to eat.

Just then, for the first time in a long while, I thought of my father, who had made me a promise: 'In three months the war will be over and then I'll get you a new bike.'

Now I had a bike, although the war still wasn't over, but I would never get one from my father.

After lunch, Kees had a nap and Clara took me upstairs to show me where I would sleep. There was an attic running the full length of the house that was divided in two by a big wooden partition. A door in this wall led to Clara's bedroom. I'd suddenly acquired a sister too!

Then she showed me around the whole house, the barn and the greenhouses. An hour later Kees appeared again.

'Why don't you give that lad a pair of clogs for his feet before anything else. Who'd let him wade through the mud in his good shoes?' he grumbled to Clara.

'So what, I'll polish them myself later,' she retorted.

I'd forgotten to bring my old work shoes. I hadn't worn clogs at Arie and Mien's, so I can't describe my amazement at this unfamiliar footwear. There were so many new impressions to take in during that one hour.

When I was alone for a moment, I hurried out to the barn and up the stairs to the loft to check if there really was a bike. And sure enough, there it was: a new bike with half-empty tyres. I was so astounded that I didn't even dare touch it. I quietly crept back down and wandered through the barn. Kees saw me and started grumbling, because grumbling was his favourite pastime. But they were the very kindest of people.

That evening we sat around in the living room, where everyone had their own chair. Including me. Mijntje and

Kees were silent, but Clara and I chatted nineteen to the dozen; we got along brilliantly. When it was time for Kees to go to bed, he looked at me and warned me not to stay up too late because we'd have to be up at six the next morning.

Not much later I went upstairs, got undressed and climbed into bed. I couldn't sleep for a long time. I just lay there comfortably, feeling content and safe. I was almost happy. I think I'd just fallen asleep when I woke up with a start. My face was damp. I didn't understand, I just turned over and went back to sleep.

The next morning Mijntje woke me up. I got dressed and had a wash under the pump in the kitchen. Our breakfast sandwiches were waiting for us, and then we went to work. In clogs. I had never walked in those things before, and although it seemed fun at first, the novelty and excitement soon wore off. It was ghastly. My clogs got sucked into the wet soil and I could hardly move. When Mijntje called me in at half past eight for a cup of coffee, I staggered inside on feet that had undergone the most dreadful torment. When I asked if I could put my normal shoes on again, Kees looked at me in complete befuddlement. A heated discussion followed and I heard Mijntje say that I should get clogs with straps, called trip clogs, but Kees thought that was nonsense. He said I'd soon get used to it.

By noon I no longer knew what feet *were*; I couldn't tell if I still had any. My poor city feet just couldn't deal with those wooden monstrosities. Indoors everyone always walked around in socks, thank goodness, and I couldn't take my clogs off quickly enough. When I had to go back out an hour later to resume my work, they had vanished and a new pair stood in their place, this time with leather straps. That made walking much easier.

That was just like Mijntje: no words, just deeds.

When I came down at half past eight the next morning for coffee and bread, Mijntje told me I had to pop to the baker's. She gave me two baking trays filled with bread dough which I was to hand over to the baker, who would put them in the oven for us. There I went, carrying those awkward tins and wearing those awkward clogs, because even with trip clogs, walking was still an uncomfortable job, if not an impossible one.

★ ★ ★

It was only at Kees and Mijntje's that I settled down and completely relaxed. I'd been very happy at Arie and Mien's, but with Mijntje and Kees I finally stopped feeling like I was in hiding, mainly because of the responsibilities Kees gave me.

★ ★ ★

As I was dragging myself over the bridge, trying to lift my feet as little as possible, I came across a few boys sitting on the railings. At that moment I became one of them, one of the village: they gave me a nickname. Everyone in the village had a nickname, and it was an honour to be given one in such a short time. I was and remained a stranger, of course, even though I had been living there for almost two years; in such a small community it would often take many years before you belonged. 'Hey Shuffles!' they called after me. 'Shuffles!'

The bakery was bustling with people, but no one needed to give their name because Mr Van Rijn, the baker, knew everybody. When it was my turn he asked me whose bread I had brought. I didn't immediately know what to say and then said my own name first, followed by the names of Kees and Mijntje. Everybody started laughing and I could feel myself shrinking. The baker said there were at least twenty people going by those names in the village, but I didn't know what else to say. I didn't even know for sure what my address was. Luckily it was no problem; I just had to come back to collect the loaves myself. Then the baker would know which tins were mine.

On the way back I crossed the bridge again and one of the boys there called out: 'Look boys, here comes Shuffles again!' When I got home no one looked up as I came in; I already belonged there too. In the kitchen I was handed a cup of tea, made just the way I liked it.

The next morning I suddenly realised that I hadn't seen any Germans for quite some time. I asked Clara if there were any Germans in Roelofarendsveen and she looked at me as if I'd gone crazy. Whatever would they want here?

* * *

A neighbour on Zuideinde, Jan Hoogeboom, told me later that the Germans had no interest in Roelofarendsveen because you could only get into it from one side; it was almost entirely surrounded by water. As the Germans didn't fancy getting caught with only one exit, they steered well clear.

That made sense to me. In my days as a tramp on the streets and canals of Amsterdam I also never went anywhere with only one way in or out. Like the Germans, I always looked for multiple escape routes.

★ ★ ★

By this time I was enjoying life and becoming quite cocky again, as befits a boy of my age. I also loved my work. I spent all day outdoors, and a certain sense of responsibility was expected of me from day one. I learned quickly and was dedicated. I often took the initiative; after all, I'd got used to doing that during my months on the streets, and they accepted it from me too, but sometimes I went too far in Kees's eyes and then he told me off, just as he would have rebuked his own son, if he'd had one.

What was more, every Sunday morning I got pocket money: two and a half guilders. They gave me the whole amount to begin with, but then I had to give one and a half

Lex and Kees planting bulbs. (Courtesy of Fiety Lesgever)

guilders back to be put aside as savings. I thought that was a very unfair system; I'd never had pocket money before, so now that I was given money only to have to hand a large part of it back, I was most indignant.

I began to rack up plenty of clothes as well. Mijntje never let on when she found a good bargain. No, instead a new shirt would suddenly appear, or new socks. I gradually came to see such things as normal again.

15

I fairly quickly acquired a whole bunch of friends.

Roelofarendsveen was a devoutly Catholic place. One Sunday morning my friend Har hesitantly brought up something that had been bothering him. His father had told him that I was a Jew-boy and he wanted to find out what that was all about. All he knew about Judaism was from the New Testament – that the Jews had crucified Jesus and that we were circumcised – and he didn't understand any of it.

I tried to explain what it meant to be a Jew but I didn't get very far either, and the end result was that both of us unbuttoned our trousers behind the bushes and comparisons were made.

'So is that the difference between a Jew and a Catholic?' he asked.

The only thing I knew to reply was, 'I guess so.'

And that was the end of that subject.

Har and I were best mates for the whole of my time in Roelofarendsveen and we were always together. One day Kees mentioned that in the spring we sometimes needed to get another farmhand, and I suggested Har. Kees wasn't too keen at first but after some discussion it was decided that I could ask him.

From then on we were practically inseparable. At ten o'clock every Sunday morning we went to church together and afterwards we went to Har's house for coffee. And then, if the weather was good enough, we would dash off to the lock and rig up Har's boat to go sailing on the Braassemermeer.

In those days I didn't know how to swim and Har's father was very worried about that. Imagine something happened to the lad, what then? A living boy in hiding wasn't so dangerous but a dead one was a different story; after all, I couldn't be buried in the Catholic graveyard. That was only for Catholics and there were no other cemeteries. We had a good laugh about it and didn't get what the problem was, but I'm certain that Mr Van de Wereld didn't like it one bit.

Har had a large family, and I often went to visit and loved it. It was great fun when we were allowed to make pancakes on the stove in the living room. I had taken to my new surroundings like a duck to water, as if the months of roaming the streets in Amsterdam had never happened. I didn't run into the *Grüne Polizei* or any Germans and I saw nothing of the war any more, although the food shortages in the rest of the Netherlands were getting pretty dire by then.

The only occasional reminder of the war was the drone of bombers flying over on their way to Germany. Then that terrible night in Ommen would come back to me, but most of the time I was too tired to think and would go straight to sleep in the evening. Yet I was still regularly woken up by drops of water on my face, and I still didn't understand why. One evening I took a ladder and inspected the roof boards but I couldn't find anything amiss. I decided to stay awake for once to find out how it came about. Late in the evening I heard someone come up the stairs very quietly and I quickly shut my eyes, but kept them open a crack so I could still see.

Mijntje crept into my room. She had a little bowl in her hands and she dipped her fingers into it. Then she made the sign of the cross above my forehead and the water dripped from her fingers.

Now the mystery might have been solved, but I couldn't think of any reason why she would do this and I didn't dare ask either. One morning I told Har about it and he started laughing. I thought he was laughing at me, but then he explained that the water was holy water and that Mijntje was blessing me every evening before she went to bed.

All these small, thoughtful gestures made me love my new family more and more and I was terribly proud to live among them. The family seemed to keep growing too. Over time I got to know more and more aunts and uncles and on my birthday the room was full of visitors. And although presents were very scarce in those days, everyone still brought a little something. Even now I find it hard to put into words what it all meant to me.

Every Sunday afternoon I also faithfully attended the services led by my friend, Father Schrama. I had become very close to him and he never tried to talk me into accepting another religion, although by the end I could sing a Latin mass from memory. And I was allowed to play the organ in the rectory and accompany the singing during Vespers.

One day Har and I came up with yet another scheme. Har earned his own money and could spend it as he wished, unlike me. I still had to put aside one guilder and fifty cents every week, and the money was kept in a soup tureen on a high shelf in the cupboard. I could have taken some cash out whenever I wanted, but I didn't have the heart even to think about doing it. In the six months that I'd been living with Kees and Mijntje, I had developed a great respect for them, and I would never have done anything to betray their trust in me.

So Har and I decided to start doing a few deals of our own, although if I'm honest it was always Har's idea. One day we had the chance to buy a row of gladioli from Mr Zaal, who was really more of a farmer than a horticulturist. The row was in a narrow strip of ground alongside a field and was priced at fifteen guilders, a sum Har could easily advance. But that was against our principles. Everything was to be split fifty–fifty, this purchase included. No problem for Har, but I had to go cap in hand to Kees for my own money, as I put it then. After I'd explained calmly and in detail what I wanted to do with the money, he allowed me to take seven and a half guilders. But when the gladioli were ready to be sold, he would be the one who took them to auction; that way he would still have some control over what we were doing. Once they'd been sold, Kees paid Har and me our money, minus the auction expenses. That's how he taught me to deal with the outside world.

One Sunday, after about seven months at Kees and Mijntje's, Har and I quickly drank our coffee at his house, told Father Schrama that we weren't coming to church, and hurried to the lakeshore to rig up the boat so we could spend the afternoon sailing on the Braassemermeer. Our provisions consisted mainly of fruit from our own fields – mostly melons or strawberries, and we'd always pick a melon that a slug had been at first so you could be sure it was a sweet one.

We were having a wonderful time sailing when at around two o'clock I got an inexplicable headache, which was so bad that it made me throw up. At first we thought I might be seasick, but it kept getting worse, so we had to go back to the shore. I was unable to walk home by then, so Har sailed to my house and moored the boat there.

I was bedridden for three days with a bucket beside me, throwing up all the time. I couldn't bear the light, so the curtains had to stay firmly closed. For the first time in my life I felt properly ill. When I came downstairs again after three days there wasn't much left of me.

From then on the headache attacks recurred at regular intervals, and when it all became too much Kees and Mijntje decided it was time for the doctor to come, but that brought some difficulties. The doctor had never had anything to do with me; he probably didn't even know I existed. I imagine Kees just told him who and especially what I was. He gave me some powders for the pain, but they didn't help one bit.

'I can't really do anything for you,' the doctor said. 'It's strange that it lasts longer than three days, but there's really nothing wrong with you.'

★ ★ ★

After the war, I went to the doctor to ask about my symptoms, and he explained why my migraines came especially on Sundays. Sunday, he told me, was the only day of the week when I was free and relaxed, so it was the only time the headaches had a chance.

★ ★ ★

A few weeks later the village crier went around on his bike, announcing his approach with a few loud bangs on his biscuit tin. This was his message: 'By order of the mayor all people in hiding must present themselves at eight o'clock this evening in the auction hall, where the mayor shall address them.'

That evening, once most of them had complied with this request, the mayor gave a thunderous speech about the behaviour of some of the people in hiding. They were so irresponsible that they were endangering the whole village. He forbade them from leaving to go into town and, even worse, from going home for the weekend. Not until he'd finished was everyone allowed to leave.

The war increasingly made itself felt in Roelofarendsveen, most obviously through the lack of things to buy. It became more and more difficult to take goods to auction because it was harder to arrange transport. One day Kees contacted his fuel supplier in Hoogmade only to be told there was no more coal. That made him angry because he had been a good customer there for many years, and now they were fobbing him off about being out of coal? That simply wasn't on. After some discussion he was offered a *praam*-load of peat – a *praam* being a kind of small barge with a sail – and when that really turned out to be the only solution, he agreed to it and asked when the peat could be delivered. To add insult to injury, he learned that he had to collect it himself, because delivery was no longer an option. That was just too much for a man who had now at last truly come face to face with the war. When talking didn't help any more, I suggested that we fetch the peat together. He looked at me in silence, then he agreed.

Hoogmade wasn't very far from de Veen, but it took a few hours by boat. On the way out the journey went smoothly, partly because the boat was empty, but on the way back everything was against us. As we travelled along the Wetering canal, which ran parallel to a long road, we saw what was going on in the rest of the world. Endless lines of people were walking down the road, looking for food. Some were pushing bicycles, others had carts or were lugging bags on their backs. It struck me how many of them were women and children, with a few elderly people here and there. We didn't really understand. Even if we didn't have enough fuel, we still had enough to eat.

At this point it also started raining quite heavily. That was no problem for the peat, but it was for father Kees. I suggested that he should take shelter under the tarpaulin and leave it to me to get the *praam* home.

I had gradually gained Kees's trust and he left me to handle things more and more. Later on that would prove to be a very good thing for both of us.

Life had taken a more normal turn for me. It was a time of war for everyone, including me, but I had gone from a real war to a somewhat subdued one. I had freedom, friends, a family, and even though it wasn't a 'real' family, it was all very real to me back then. They might not have been my parents, but they treated me like their son.

One day, at the end of September 1944, Kees said we had to go and lift potatoes. I didn't even know that we still had potatoes anywhere. It turned out that for many years Kees had leased a piece of land from another farmer. It was on the other side of the Braassemermeer, in the Vierambachtspolder, and he planted potatoes on it every year to be eaten at home.

Kees and I crossed over in the rowing boat, armed with a pair of pitchforks. On the second day Kees fell ill and started to cough a lot. When we got home he had a little to eat and then went straight to bed, assuming he'd be well again the following day. Mijntje and I both said it might be wiser if he took it easy with some lighter work around the house, but he still got up the next morning to cross the lake with me again.

The coughing got worse during the course of the day and at three o'clock I said it would be madness to go on and that we were going home. Kees barely even protested. It was scary to see how ill he was and on the way back I watched him get worse still. The crossing took about three-quarters of an hour and I couldn't row quickly enough to get him home and in bed as soon as possible. He didn't even bother to get the boat through the lock himself, a task he'd never normally leave to me.

I tied the boat to the post at the edge of the canal and took him home. Mijntje put him to bed with a big pile of blankets on top, but he couldn't stop shivering from the cold. He got sicker by the hour and started sweating terribly. We weren't sure what we could do to help him.

Very early the next morning I went to fetch the doctor, and then I really had to go back to the Vierambachtspolder to harvest the rest of the potatoes, but I didn't manage to get them all into the *praam*. By the time I came home in the early evening, the doctor had come out and it seemed that Kees's condition had worsened. Mijntje and I sat with him all night. He had been given several medicines but we could see no improvement yet.

I couldn't go back to salvage the remaining potatoes the following day, because overnight the city-boy had to start running the horticultural business. Kees was far too ill for that. He had pneumonia, very risky in those days. It meant he would be out of the picture for six weeks for sure, and even then only with luck. Everybody around me saw it as normal that I was now making the decisions, without being able to ask anyone for advice.

This was the start of a pretty tough time for me, because during the day I had to work extra hard and at night I took turns to sit with Kees. The doctor visited every day and when the illness was at its peak he came twice. One day the priest even came to anoint him, the last rites that would prepare Kees for death and his transition to the afterlife.

There was nothing for it now but to go and harvest the rest of the potatoes, even though the weather forecast was bad and I was still very tired. Armed with some jute sacks, a couple of bulkhead boards to help load the *praam* to its maximum capacity and a few square metres of tarpaulin, I set off very early. I had arranged to borrow the farmer's horse and cart for the day to move the potatoes to the boat. The sky looked more threatening by the minute, and the farmer helped me out by leading the horse, which I was scared to death of, to the boat. Together we managed to get the harvest into the *praam* before it started raining.

At three o'clock I set off back across the lake, the boat sitting low in the water. The bulkheads were in place and the sacks were squeezed into the gaps between the boards and the boat to make sure as little water as possible got in. I'd only just started out when I felt the first raindrops. Besides the small sail I also had oars, of course, and I used them to gain more speed. In the middle of the lake the wind started to blow harder, but unfortunately from the wrong direction. I had tremendous difficulty keeping the boat on course, as I needed to reach the lock.

All of a sudden the wind picked up so fiercely that I got into trouble. The waves were so high that they sloshed into the boat and I got really scared. I decided to take down the sail and let the wind push the boat to let in less water. That helped, but I completely lost course. I tried to work out where I would end up, but because of the storm I had no idea where I was, let alone where I would land. Feeling sure that if something happened to the boat I was certain to drown, I went and sat at the very back with the oars across my lap. If the boat sank, I would at least have something to keep me afloat.

All kinds of thoughts went through my head. Had I done my utmost to stay alive only to drown in this stupid lake? More and more water came into the boat and I just let the wind push me wherever. One thing was certain: I had gone a long way past the lock.

Just when I thought that I was about to go down with the boat, potatoes and all, the shore suddenly loomed up. I heard voices shouting and felt the boat being pulled firmly from all sides. It was pitch black by now, so I felt more than saw a pair of big hands pulling me out of the boat, while others moored it. I had landed in Oude Wetering.

Once again I had been lucky, and once again people had stood ready to help me.

At home they were all beside themselves. Not only had my crossing taken an hour longer than normal, but it was also at least an hour's walk from Oude Wetering to Zuideinde in Roelofarendsveen, so you can imagine how late I got home. I was so thoroughly wet and cold that Mijntje put me straight to bed and fed me my meal there. She had been terribly worried. Once I'd eaten, I slept like a log. I was absolutely exhausted. Mijntje let me sleep till three o'clock and then it was my turn to keep watch at Kees's bedside. He just wasn't getting better.

Food was becoming scarcer for us, too, and the peat burnt much quicker than we had hoped. Now the war was real here too. No light, less food and no fuel.

We decided to cut down one of the chestnut trees in front of the house. I couldn't manage it on my own, of course – I needed help. There was no lack of assistance but very little expertise. When we started, my helpers thought we needed to get the tree out roots and all. I totally disagreed because the ground was soft peat, and that was bound to cause problems. The tree was at least 80 years old, so it had extensive roots, and it was so close to the house that most of them were probably underneath the foundations. But of course, they thought a city-boy had no idea about these things, so the tree wasn't cut down with a saw but was wholly uprooted.

It went well, and once the tree had been sawn into pieces we had easily enough wood for a year. But the ground had been disturbed by the removal of the roots, and as a result that corner of the house had such bad subsidence that the groundwater came up into the living room!

Just when we thought Kees couldn't get any worse, he fortunately started to improve, little by little. But he didn't seem to gain any strength. The food he needed wasn't available, and so all he could do for a long time was watch as the city-boy did all the work, which didn't really help his recovery.

16

5 May 1945

It was a beautiful spring day, a good reason for Kees to venture out again, and we decided to give the front garden a thorough going-over together. That's how he put it. I did the heavy work while he squatted and stuck some annuals in the ground. It clearly did him good to be outside and have something to do; his whole life had been spent outdoors, after all.

To our surprise, we saw a lot of people in the street waving red, white and blue flags. We'd got used to all sorts of things by then, but this definitely struck us as odd. There were two men we didn't know trying to ride bikes, without much success. Then Gerard Koning, our neighbour from across the way, walked by. We asked him what was going on and he told us that the war was over. We had no idea! We didn't have a clandestine radio and never went to listen at anyone else's house either. We dropped what we were doing in the garden and rushed inside to tell the others.

I was terribly glad, but in the background was a feeling of fear that was hard to describe. Fear of the unknown. In the days that followed I began to realise that something would have to be done with me, but I had no idea what. We had suddenly gone back to normal times.

Over the last several months I had lived a fairly carefree existence. Prior to that I'd had fears and worries, of course, but that was very different. Now I was responsible for a business and worried about a man who had been seriously ill. It was a heavy burden and I fretted over it quite a bit, but when I finished work in the evening and came indoors I felt an enormous warmth and security. This was where I belonged. Strangely enough, I'd found my place thanks to the war.

And now the war was over, the Germans were gone. I was free to come and go wherever I wanted, but all of a sudden I didn't know where I stood or where I wanted to go. There was no longer any need to stay put. Nobody would send me away, of course, but could I still take advantage of their hospitality?

All these thoughts kept turning round and round during the first days after the liberation, but I was only thinking with my head and not with my heart. Time passed and we soon had enough to eat again. Har and I were pretty good at doing deals with the English and Canadian soldiers. We traded strawberries and other produce for goods that they had but we didn't, like chocolate and cigarettes. In this way we both provided for our respective families.

As time went by I increasingly began to long for Amsterdam, or rather for my parents and the rest of my family. I couldn't expect much help from Mijntje and Kees because they knew even less about such matters than I did, so when I brought it up one evening over dinner, everyone at the table was shocked. Clearly I hadn't been the only one to keep reality at arm's length during these first weeks of euphoria; they also hadn't wanted to face up to what liberation might mean.

Of course I wanted more than anything to go back to live with my father and mother and see my brothers again, but inside my head there was such chaos. Nor was there anyone I could talk to about these things, and maybe I didn't want to either. I simply had no idea what to do. I didn't dare take any action; I felt caught in a huge dilemma, and maybe even a conflict of loyalties. It was not just a question of having to leave my new family, but also whether I even wanted to go in the first place. In hindsight I think I was already subconsciously afraid of what I might find out. But I had to do something and decided to go to Amsterdam for the day.

When I told Mijntje and Kees about my decision, they quite understood that I had to do it, though they thought I was being hasty. But I insisted, and on the day of my departure they made me some sandwiches and pressed some money into my hands, without me having asked for it.

I got a lift with the van that transported vegetables into town, which meant I was already in Amsterdam by eight in the morning. When I got out of the van I had no idea where I was; I was utterly disorientated. I grabbed a passer-by and asked for directions to my old neighbourhood, Jodenbreestraat. It was more than an hour's walk and what I found there left me crestfallen.

Most houses were occupied by strangers or had been half-demolished because people had taken out the wood during the Hunger Winter, as was the case with my family home.

Wood from houses demolished during the Hunger Winter in Jodenbreestraat. (Beeldbank WO2/Resistance Museum, Amsterdam/G.H. Krüger)

Wandering about on all sides were dazed people who, like me, were searching for something which no longer existed.

Drifting through my old neighbourhood, I felt that I had lost everything. The sight of this pitiful place, which had once been so warm and friendly, was appalling. I hadn't cried for a long time, but now the tears rolled down my cheeks. An awful reality began to sink in; my dreamland of the last few weeks evaporated. I had unconsciously entertained hopes which were now suddenly dashed. I realised that my wonderful time in Roelofarendsveen had only been a temporary solution, and I saw that the months I spent roaming the streets in Amsterdam had been but a prelude of what was to come. I also understood that I could not cope alone with what now lay ahead of me, but I didn't have the faintest idea where to start. There was only one thing left for me to do: quickly go back to the safety of de Veen. I didn't know whether to laugh or cry.

When I got back, Mijntje, Kees and Clara were waiting for me in the living room and looked at me questioningly, saying nothing, but I could hardly utter a word. I tried to explain what I had seen, but of course they didn't know my old surroundings. They'd never encountered dispossession like this before. That whole night I did nothing but cry.

The next morning we went to the polder to cut peonies, and when we went to the shed at half past ten for our coffee, Kees cleared his throat. He said he couldn't help me because he didn't know what I should do either, but he knew one thing for certain and I shouldn't forget it: I could stay with them for the rest of my life. For them, the end of the war was not the end of our bond. He added that maybe it would be wise to have a chat with the notary. He advised everyone – he would know what I should do.

A few weeks after the liberation, the first newspapers reappeared and news from the outside world landed on our doormat. The reports we received were too many and too horrifying to take in. We read about concentration camps where countless Jews had been murdered. At that point they still didn't know how many, but it was clear that the numbers were very high. Some survivors from the camps had been sent to Sweden and Switzerland, so there was still a glimmer of hope.

Kees made an appointment with the notary and I went to see him. I took a seat in front of his desk and he talked to me very kindly. Because of that gentleness I assumed he had bad news for me, but he didn't go that far. No, he couldn't tell me anything definite, but he had found out how I should best proceed.

Following his advice, I went back to Amsterdam, but this time with a few addresses in my pocket where I could ask for help. First I had to report to an organisation which kept records of people who had not been deported. The first person I met was Mr Druif, our neighbour who used to live on Zandstraat. He looked at me and said, 'I know you!' I had to wait a while so I joined him at his little table. He asked what I was going to do now and I told him I really didn't know. I was 16 years old – how could I give a sensible answer to a question like that?

'Then I do. You'll be going to the boys' orphanage, no two ways about it,' he said.

I tried to defend myself because I definitely didn't want that, so I said, 'But when my parents come back I'll go to live with them again, surely?'

He looked at me with pity and replied that the chance of them coming back was very small, and while I was waiting for them I would certainly go to the orphanage.

People trying to interfere in my life again, I grumbled to myself, and I recalled what Kees had said that morning in the shed.

Then it was my turn and a very nice lady bombarded me with questions, most of which I couldn't answer. She ran her finger down a very long list of names and after a while she said that my family wasn't on the list of survivors yet, but that new lists were arriving every day and she would keep an eye out for me. She asked me to give her my address so she could let me know as soon as there was any news.

'Do you have any possessions? Or any money?'

I told her I'd saved some of my pocket money.

'Who gave you pocket money?' she asked in surprise.

Now it was my turn to look surprised. I told her how I had been living over the last few years and she began to laugh.

'You've been very lucky indeed.'

After this discussion I went straight back home. There was no other reason for me to be in Amsterdam for the time being. When we had supper that evening, I got a cooked dinner instead of sandwiches. I looked at Mijntje in surprise and she said, 'Well, you didn't have a proper meal at lunchtime.' A true mother speaking.

After supper everyone listened carefully while I told them about my day, and when Clara heard that I might have to go into an orphanage, she said I'd be better off just living at home. As far as she was concerned, this was my home. 'You're not going to the big city,' she said, and that was the end of the discussion for her.

Days and weeks went by, but no message came about my family, and slowly but irrevocably the tragedy began to sink in. I didn't dare talk about it with anyone, much as I wanted to.

Then a letter arrived from Amsterdam. I will never forget those lines; they will always be with me:

> We have been informed by the Red Cross that the following people have perished in …

… and then came the infamous camps and the names of every member of my family.

That was when it really came true. I had to face the fact that my whole world had collapsed.

17

A few days later, another letter arrived from Amsterdam which said that I had to report to Johannes Vermeerstraat because accommodation had been found for me. I would be admitted to the orphanage because I had no family left at all. When I showed it to Kees, he just shrugged and said nothing more than what he had already told me.

I didn't reply to the letter and they left me alone for a while. Then another one arrived, a little less friendly in tone. It said that I really had to present myself now as the institution had been awarded guardianship over me and was therefore going to house me. I discussed this with my other adviser, Mr De Jong from Leiden, who said that I should come to stay with him for a while, without leaving an address behind.

★ ★ ★

A few weeks after the liberation I joined Mr De Jong for the first time. Mr De Jong had a decorating business on the Nieuwe Rijn in Leiden. He'd had to go into hiding because of his underground activities and had come to live, like so many others, in de Veen. During his two years there he had

built a fabulous houseboat called The Gull. *After the war I
helped him tow it to a beautiful mooring near Kaag.*

★ ★ ★

So in fact I had to go into hiding for a second time. For a
while the orphanage tried its best to find me, but then left
me alone and I could return to my own familiar old home
on Zuideinde.

But I got more and more restless, I didn't even feel settled
in de Veen any more, but where would I feel settled? I decided
to go to Amsterdam a bit more often to see how other people
were carrying on with their lives. I made up my mind to
spend the weekend there. What I would do when I got there
I didn't yet know, but in any case I had to try. I chose to go at
the weekend as my work on the farm would suffer least that
way, because that was gnawing at me too. I had come to love
my work, but I felt I had to choose for myself as well.

Back in Amsterdam, I wandered through my old neighbourhood and met more and more people looking for
the same things as me; they didn't seem to know how or
where to begin either. Most, like me, were totally alone in
the world. If you'd survived with other members of your
family then everything was very different. The aid for families was much more effective than for people on their own.

I was looking around on Valkenburgerstraat when a lady
I knew tapped me on the arm. She told me about Jannie,
a second cousin of mine, who had also come back, and
she gave me an address where I could find her. We were

family, but we'd not had much contact in the past. She was a few years older than me and was staying with friends for a while, but she was high on the list to get a place of her own. It turned out she was in a relationship with a good friend of Wolf's. She arranged for me to stay with an acquaintance of hers for the weekend. That was a start.

In this way I spent some time building up contacts and at the end of September I moved back to Amsterdam for real. I now had a small room at Jannie's new place, which she shared with her boyfriend. My savings were starting to run out so I had to find an income one way or another.

I let the relevant organisations know and they sent me to an office on Herengracht. I told them my story and they immediately helped me out by giving me an allowance of ten guilders every fortnight – too little to live on, but slightly too much to die on.

★ ★ ★

We were treated in a very indifferent and incompetent manner by the government of the day. There was definitely a difference between those they did and didn't help. I'd have been much better off if I were Catholic. This has nothing to do with what I think of Catholicism; it's about the people who practised it. What a difference between the Catholic government and the Catholic village that took me in!

★ ★ ★

A new rule was brought in which said that exceptions should be made in emergency cases, and I was such an emergency case. I didn't have a bed to sleep in so I'd been sleeping on the floor. Armed with a note allocating me a mattress and a handcart, I went to the back of Central Station, where I'd been told I could collect a mattress if I showed them the note. After two hours, when my turn finally came, an incredibly dirty specimen was thrown onto my cart and off I could go. I pushed my cart to the river IJ and tipped the filthy mattress into the water. Then I set off home with the empty cart.

During that first year after the war I did my best to bring some order into my life, but I needed a better income for that. Jannie's boyfriend helped me get a job at Maison Moderne, the fur business on Kalverstraat where Wolf had been an apprentice. I started as a junior salesman and that was a reasonably good beginning, because I was earning ten guilders a week. Everything that helped me hold on to my independence, I grabbed with both hands. I knew what work meant; I had learned that in Roelofarendsveen.

Slowly I built up a circle of acquaintances and even got to know a nice girl from work, whom I was allowed to visit at home regularly. She had a very warm and friendly family; she lived with her mother, who was divorced from her father, and two sisters. Music was the focus of their lives and that was hugely appealing to me. Her mother spoiled me in her own way, so I loved being there and went often.

★ ★ ★

The only odd thing in that period was that whenever I sat down, I could easily just fall asleep. That certainly wasn't normal for a 16-year-old boy, but the fact was that I often felt very tired and lethargic. Once, on a visit to de Veen, they tried to convince me that it was the city air, which was obviously much worse than in the country, and that I'd be much better off moving back home.

★ ★ ★

One day I fell off my bike and had to spend a few days in bed. After about three days I had a hefty coughing fit, and when I tried to clear my lungs with a few big coughs my hand was suddenly covered in blood. A few hours later the doctor was at my bedside to examine me. When he listened to my lungs he looked very troubled and said that the next day someone from the municipal health service would drop by.

Sure enough, the next day a nurse came round and took a seat at the end of my bed. First she looked at me closely and then started asking me a whole ream of questions.

'Are your parents still alive?'

'No,' I replied curtly.

'When did they die?'

'Don't know.'

'What did they die of?'

'Being Jewish.'

'Where did they die?'

'In a camp.'

'What did they die of?'

'Gas.'

'Do you have any brothers or sisters?'

'They're dead too.'

'What did they die of?'

To me, that woman was utterly insane. The form had to be filled in completely, no exceptions. Apparently she only read forms, not newspapers. She told me I had to go to a lung specialist on Nieuwe Achtergracht who would take some x-rays. They would give me a blood test and take a sample of sputum, for which she left me a special little pot, and then the result would come soon.

Well, the result did come soon, very soon. Tuberculosis in both lungs.

★　★　★

After the war there were a lot of cases of tuberculosis. Lack of food and physical exhaustion had made the population extremely susceptible. Someone only had to cough in an overcrowded tram and you were infected. In those early post-war years there were far more tuberculosis patients than the sanatoriums could cope with.

★　★　★

I was put on a waiting list for treatment and after two months I was admitted as a priority case to the Zonnestraal ('Sunbeam') sanatorium in Hilversum. As a child I had once visited the children's holiday camp run by the Friedman Foundation in Hilversum. After the war the building had been converted into a branch of the Zonnestraal sanatorium, and ironically the ward I ended up on was the dormitory I had slept in the first time round.

I had to stay in bed twenty-four hours a day. The windows and doors were kept open all day and all night, as

The Friedman Foundation, where Lex went on holiday as a child and after the war was treated for tuberculosis. (Jewish Museum, Amsterdam/Collection Jaap van Velzen)

Lex in the sanatorium. (Courtesy of Fiety Lesgever)

at the time they thought that fresh air was part of the cure. If the weather at all permitted it you would even be wheeled out, bed and all, straight after breakfast, and you'd be lying outside from early in the morning until late in the evening.

Doctor Bierhorst, my doctor and also the medical director, hoped I'd be cured in eighteen months, given my age. I was 17 when I was admitted and I have never been as desperately lonely anywhere as I was there. Everyone else had family who visited three times a week and brought all sorts of things. How often did I regret having so cleverly evaded the clutches of the Germans! The patients around me were all very kind and friendly and often shared their treats with me, but I felt deeply unhappy.

Arie and Mien, and Mijntje, Kees and Clara did drop in occasionally, but their work didn't allow them to take much time off; they had their hands full getting everything going again after the war. And I had sporadic visits from the public authority of which I was a ward. One day a lady came and told me that if I needed anything I should get in touch, and then they would see to it that my wishes were fulfilled, if possible. Well, that wasn't too hard; I had quite a few wishes. To start with I was very keen to get rid of my institutional pyjamas, because they alone made it obvious that I was a misfit pauper.

★ ★ ★

When I came of age, I had to appear before the sub-district court to dissolve the guardianship, and the judge told me I still had a savings account. He also told me that the money in the account had come from benefit payments and that I could now dispose of it as I chose.

As soon as I left the court I checked how much money I had and there, on Weteringschans, I found out that all the wishes I had been allowed to make in the sanatorium had been paid for out of my own meagre resources. I was just as penniless as I'd been before.

★ ★ ★

My recovery was not exactly a quick one: it was two years before I was finally allowed out of bed, and then I moved to a cabin in the woods. It was a kind of one-man hut measuring 2m x 2m, with an 80cm x 180cm bed, a 60cm x 60cm table, a chair and a cupboard. The side walls of the hut were glass windows that could be opened. The back was closed and the front was completely open, with a pair of saloon doors that were just 80cm tall.

This was my abode during summer and winter, and so it sometimes happened that I'd be woken up on a spring morning by a bird pecking fluff out of my blanket to build its nest. In winter it could drop to ten degrees below zero, and then my blanket would be frozen stiff. I washed in the washhouse, which I could only get to by wading for quite a distance through the snow. In pyjamas. The washhouse resembled a barracks and had a big black stove which glowed red-hot in winter. But however cold it got, I can't recall ever having been ill there.

After four and a half years, in 1952, I finally left the sanatorium, though I still hadn't fully recovered. The few

Lex's lodgings at the sanatorium. (Courtesy of Fiety Lesgever)

medicines available in those days didn't help me enough. After an initial pleasant stay with acquaintances I quite soon found a room in Amsterdam. I was invited to dinner regularly and I'd also been getting a bit of money from the *Wiedergutmachung*, the 'reparation' payments from Germany. Nothing at all came from the Dutch authorities.

Every three months I had to go to the public health office for a check-up, where they took more x-rays. Things were already amiss at the second check-up. In fact, I needed to be readmitted, but I categorically refused to be locked away again. There was quite a fight with the lung specialist. I rejected every proposal; I would rather have died.

My situation was discussed in a meeting between a number of doctors. One of them was Dr Van Lier. Because he was Jewish, he asked the doctor who was treating me if he could take me on as his patient. He told me later that he'd had to explain what the reason was, because in those years they still weren't very good at treating victims of the war, which is what I was, of course.

Luckily Dr Van Lier had enough psychological insight to be able to change my mind and we decided to operate on my lungs. In the early 1950s that was quite a major operation that certainly wasn't risk-free; not many surgeons were able to do it. At my request I was transferred to a Jewish hospital, because if I had to die then it should at least be in a place of my choice, thank you very much.

Everyone knew that my chances weren't very good, including me, so I cancelled the lease for my room and even had my name removed from the population register.

To everyone's surprise, and certainly much to my own, I survived the operation, and after some time in intensive care I was well enough to be transferred to a ward and receive visitors again. A good friend, Jan de Krijger, soon popped in and brought a colleague from the diamond-cutting workshop with him, a lovely girl called Sonja Peereboom.

The better I got, the more infrequent Jan's visits became, but Sonja came more and more often (Jan was probably well aware that Sonja and I had really hit it off) and, when I was discharged, the friendship between Sonja and me gradually turned into something else. I was invited to dinner by her parents more and more often, and although they were worried about my tuberculosis at first – they wanted to make absolutely sure that I wouldn't infect their daughter – we got their blessing in the end.

The tuberculosis caused me other problems as well, namely when looking for a job. Former tuberculosis patients didn't enjoy a great deal of protection in the 1950s. Jacques Peereboom, a distant relative of Sonja's, helped me get a job at Gerzon Brothers, a fashion retailer on Kalverstraat.

I can remember when Sonja and I got engaged as if it happened yesterday. There was no money. We had to save every penny for the rings because borrowing was out of the question. But eventually our wedding day came and we moved in with Sonja's parents. To crown our happy life, our daughter was born in 1956.

At last I was no longer alone.

I think I was one of the first fathers to be seen pushing a pram down the street on Sunday mornings. I was so madly proud of my beautiful daughter that I wanted to show her to everybody, never mind their strange looks. Everything was going Sonja's and my way; we were admittedly still living with her parents, but we could even go on holiday together!

Maybe the shock of what was to follow hit me all the harder because I was so happy. During that wonderful holiday, when we'd had our dinner and were enjoying the lovely evening, I suddenly started coughing. When I took my hand from my mouth, I was shocked to see blood spots in my white handkerchief.

I went to bed early and in the morning I called my lung specialist in Amsterdam. I had to go and see him for a check-up immediately, but he couldn't find anything wrong. He told me to take it easy for a few weeks and then we'd see.

But a few weeks later things went wrong yet again. I was laughing at a joke when I had a coughing fit accompanied

Lex and Sonja's wedding photo. (Courtesy of Fiety Lesgever)

Lex with baby Fiety. (Courtesy of Fiety Lesgever)

by a huge wave of blood, and before I knew it I was back in hospital. My health certainly wasn't getting any better, but nobody knew what was wrong with me, other than that it wasn't tuberculosis.

Fortunately they let me go home again at the end of the week, and a week after that I was back at work, because try as they might, they couldn't find the cause of my illness. But a few days later it struck again.

Feeling very low, I was admitted to hospital at Onze Lieve Vrouwe Gasthuis, where a whole team stood ready to figure out once and for all what exactly was wrong with me. The torturous examinations that I had to undergo in the weeks that followed defy description. Needles were stuck into me, tubes were inserted into my lungs and, to cap it all, oil was poured into them to improve the clarity of the x-rays. When I think back to that last procedure, my stomach still turns even now.

But it was all to no avail. Not one test provided an answer. At my wit's end, I suggested that they should just cut me open to find out what the matter was. To my surprise, my proposal wasn't immediately brushed aside; in fact, they'd already seriously contemplated it, but the only two doctors who were qualified to undertake such major surgery were away at a conference in America.

As soon as the two gentlemen landed on Dutch soil again, I was referred to them as a matter of urgency. They thought the operation would be risky, but they also realised that doing nothing wasn't an option because I was dying anyway. Only the anaesthetist objected; he didn't want the responsibility because he suspected that the strong sedation would be too much for me.

'Listen,' I said, 'I'm tired. If it were only about me, I'd tell you to let me quietly slip away. But it's no longer just about me. I have a wife and an angel of a daughter. I want to live for them.'

This argument got the anaesthetist on board and the operation was scheduled for the following day. I unbuttoned my pyjama top and pointed to the spot where I thought the problem was, where all the blood seemed to be coming from. Later it turned out that this clue had helped them a great deal: they'd started looking there and soon found a cavity where the lung tissue was being eaten away, causing the heavy blood loss. The doctors had to remove nearly all of my right lung, but I fortunately recovered quickly and after about a month I was back at work.

Life was smiling on me and mine again.

From a societal point of view, the early 1960s went well for us too. My wife and I worked hard because we still needed so many things. But everything we took on seemed to work out and things got better all the time. In 1968 I was offered a good job outside Amsterdam, so once again the three of us climbed a few steps higher on the social ladder. We moved to a splendid apartment in a small but beautiful spot near Leiden, where the three of us soon found our feet. My daughter made a fresh start in secondary school and quickly made a new set of friends.

★ ★ ★

That was the time when, to my great joy, we got back in touch with the people in de Veen. Over the years we had

Lex with his daughter in the dunes. (Courtesy of Fiety Lesgever)

increasingly lost sight of each other as I'd been so intensely focused on building a life of my own, as well as overcoming my lung problems. When Sonja and I moved near Leiden, we happily became very close to the Veenders again, and so it has always remained.

★ ★ ★

After two years my income was so good that we considered buying a home of our own. In the old part of the village we found a beautiful and affordable house. Our progress was almost unstoppable. I was very happy in my work, although being responsible for forty employees weighed heavily sometimes. As a result I often worked around eighty hours a week.

In 1970 my father-in-law died, and I lost not just a father but also a friend. He was the first member of my family that I was able to bury myself after the war. But as if it had been an omen, fate struck again: in 1976 my dear Sonja fell incurably ill. The world around us collapsed, and I would happily have gone back to the air raid shelter if all this could be taken away. But there was nothing to be done. We couldn't flee from this.

A year of fighting and of trying all sorts of things followed, but nothing worked. And then, after I had sat by her hospital bedside for three days, Sonja closed her eyes for good, and my way home had never been so long. Once I got home, I sank down in the hall on the bottom step of the stairs and had a terrible row with the Lord. I called him all the names I could think of. I don't know what happened over the following twenty-four hours; my memory is a blank.

After the funeral, when my daughter and I were walking down the street together and I was taking stock, I had to admit that I felt almost as destitute as I had thirty-three years before. *Almost*, because I had her now, thank God. This was the start of a hard time. My work didn't interest me any more and I would have liked to call it a day, but nothing was more difficult than that. I had fought my whole life – it had become second nature – so after a while I picked up the pieces and carried on.

18

What is harder than looking back, when you are used to always looking ahead?

Humans are not made to go through life alone, and a year and a half after Sonja's death I met a woman, Corrie, whom I later married. Because we were both from the world of commerce, I decided to give up my job in Leiden and start a business with my new life partner on one of the most expensive streets in

Lex in 2014. (Courtesy of Fiety Lesgever)

Amsterdam. We got on well together from the start and I was very happy with her, as were the people close to me.

Corrie was from quite a large family and one of her brothers lived in Germany with his wife. My wife understood better than anyone that I had to brace myself when I met this couple for the first time, in the summer of 1979.

They invited us to come and stay with them in Germany, and Corrie was very surprised when I accepted the invitation. Knowing that I would find it very difficult to go to Germany, she kept postponing the visit. Yet the moment finally came for us to go and I looked at the road atlas for directions.

That was when I discovered that they lived pretty close to the concentration camp of Bergen-Belsen, and an idea briefly came into my mind which I instantly dismissed. Why should I look for problems? What did I want to do in that camp? I tried to forget about it but the idea had taken hold of me.

After days of fretting, I decided to mention the plan to my wife. She was terribly shocked and asked if I couldn't be dissuaded, but my decision was made. 'OK', she said, 'if you really feel you have to, we'll go together.' She was equally shocked by my reaction to that suggestion. I wanted to go to Bergen-Belsen on my own.

Dirk and Thea lived less than an hour's drive from the camp and my wife was dreading the impact that the confrontation would have. After all, the name Bergen-Belsen alone made me shudder.

In August 1984 I spent many days in the Amsterdam Municipal Archives looking up the names of every member of my family, before going to the NIOD, the Institute for War, Holocaust and Genocide Studies, on Herengracht.

There I found the names with their dates of death and the camps where they were murdered.

As chance would have it, no one in my family had been transported to Bergen-Belsen, and yet that was where I was going, of all places. But what difference did it make? None of them had come back; they were among the six million Jewish victims whom the Germans had murdered in ghettos, in countless massacres and in a whole system of camps.

And so I was going to visit one of the most notorious concentration camps.

★ ★ ★

I tried to imagine what I would find there, and I doubted whether I could cope with it. Normally I could control my feelings, but I really didn't know if I could handle this. What had got into me to do this, when I'd once been near Westerbork and hadn't had the courage to actually visit? Was I perhaps ashamed to show my face there? I, who had made such an effort to escape with my life, while all those others hadn't stood a chance and were therefore no longer with us? Shouldn't I too have walked the 'Boulevard des Misères', and was I now ashamed that I hadn't done so? There is no answer to such questions.

Years after the war I still felt shame whenever I enjoyed myself or had a good laugh about something. You felt that wasn't on. You felt ashamed because of those who hadn't survived the war. Having fun was so banal. That made the guilt much worse.

★ ★ ★

How much stronger would these feelings of guilt be on my visit to the concentration camp? I tried to banish such thoughts from my mind, but every muscle in my body tensed up and I locked myself away in my study for hours on end.

One day, in September 1984, my wife called me downstairs. She had made coffee, knowing that was the way to entice me out of my room. It was nearly eight o'clock, time for the news, and to my shame I had to admit that the images, however dreadful, of the former Yugoslavia, now ravaged by war, began to appear commonplace; everyone was becoming somewhat immune to them. It seemed like 1936 all over again, when Hitler started to prepare his people for the biggest genocide in history. Now the victims have different names and are mostly small groups, but what the TV shows us and what the papers describe are only the tip of the iceberg.

Now 'foreigners' are on the receiving end and get blamed for everything instead of the Jews. Now it's the Turks and the Moroccans who are held responsible for the difficult economic situation in the Netherlands. There are quite simply bad eggs in our society; the world will never be free of them. They'll always be there, wherever you go. I got up and switched the television off, thinking to myself that I couldn't do anything about it anyway. But that's exactly where the danger lurks; that's what all the other millions of people think too.

I called my brother-in-law Dirk to arrange a date for our visit. It had to be postponed another few weeks until after Rosh Hashanah, but we fixed our stay for the first week of October 1985.

After I went to bed, the doubts started again. To go or not to go? Was I still so sure that I wanted to visit Bergen-Belsen? The doubts lingered, but I decided that nothing or no one would stop me if I made up my mind to go.

The next day I took the map and drew a red circle around the two settlements that together made up Bergen-Belsen. I sat in silence, staring at the two names. Maybe Corrie was right and I was mad to do this. I couldn't even watch a film about the Holocaust, and now I wanted to seek it out?

But by that point I'd become so obsessed with the journey that I really began to grimly look forward to it, and at last the day came for us to leave for Germany. We did a bit of shopping in the morning and once we'd put the Dutch cheese and packs of coffee in the car, we set off at about noon, aiming to get to Rehburg by five o'clock.

I'm not sure anyone could tell, but I was walking around feeling like I had a brick in my stomach. That evening, Thea, my sister-in-law, gave me directions to Bergen-Belsen. She, too, offered to come with me but I firmly declined. It was starting to look like some sort of self-flagellation.

I woke very early the next day and jumped out of bed straight away, because sleep was now out of the question. The ominous feeling that came over me was familiar – I recognised it from the past. That sixth sense which used to warn me when something unpleasant was about to happen during the war years had reawakened in all its intensity.

After breakfast it was time to go, but I was suddenly no longer in such a hurry. I mooched around for a bit and had to force myself to leave. The route took me via Linsburg and Essel. At least it was a beautiful sunny day, even warm for the time of year. On another occasion, in another country, in different surroundings, it would have been a lovely day out.

It was still very early and the little villages I passed through were all sleepy and peaceful. As soon as I left one, I entered another, because despite the rural surroundings, it still was rather densely populated. I made slower and slower progress, I was dawdling more and more without realising it, and when I left Winsen and immediately entered the village of Walle, my heart almost stopped. Taking a left turn, I came upon a big white arrow and underneath it the words *Gedenkstätte Bergen-Belsen*.

Just seeing the sign cut me to the quick. I slammed my foot on the brake and pulled over on the side of the road. I was gasping for breath and went all cold and clammy. All my muscles tensed up as if I had to fight or flee. And of course that was essentially the case.

After a few minutes I started quietly talking to myself, telling myself to calm down. I sat there for at least ten minutes before starting the car again and driving the last few hundred metres.

Now the camp was in front of me. Neat new buildings stood in front of the renovated entrance. There were a dozen or so cars in the large car park. Feeling a little numb, I pulled up, switched off the engine and sat staring at that big, tall gate, which might well have been new but didn't look any less terrifying. I sat there and the tears rolled slowly down my cheeks.

I couldn't think or see or feel anything else; I could only weep and didn't know how to stop.

For at least fifteen minutes I sat there like that, looking at that imposing gate, which you couldn't climb over, even now. They'd probably kept to the original size when they made it; maybe they'd even used architectural drawings from back then.

I got out and felt my knees trembling underneath me. I walked unsteadily into a building where all sorts of documentation was available to take or buy. I was offered a map of the camp, but I had no need for anything like that.

I stepped through a door and entered the camp itself, with neatly laid paths. After only ten steps my brain threw in the towel and I walked on feeling totally numb. After a hundred metres I stopped by a large flat boulder with a map on it. Beyond it I looked out over a big open area with memorial stones here and there. Like a robot I walked along the neat paths to the first mass grave, where a sign said that here lay 1,500 dead. Nameless. One thousand five hundred nameless people, humiliated, tortured, mentally and physically violated, and finally left to die in agony and squalor.

An icy chill ran through me and I buttoned up my jacket. A cold wind seemed to blow across the expanse that froze you to the bone, and which hadn't been there outside the camp. A sinister place, where even the temperature felt sinister.

I walked and walked and came upon a place where thousands of people had had to stand on roll call for hours on end. For a long while I stood motionless in a fruitless attempt to feel what I had been spared. Just then I had been in de Veen, having a good life.

There I stood, overwhelmed by shame. On that spot I understood that the sense of guilt that had taken root in us, the survivors, was well founded. Even if you'd known how your own deportation would have ended.

Once again I wept, and once again I didn't try to hold back the tears, because anyone who doesn't cry in that place is making a pointless visit. I sat down on a circular bench where they, the dead, had been forced to keep standing, a cruel joke. When I got up at last to go on, I was so frozen that I made my way to the exit. After leaving the camp I went to my car and noticed the warmth of the

sun on my back. It really was a more pleasant temperature than it had been inside, although I know it was just
my imagination.

I sat immobile, staring blindly ahead. After a while,
having wiped away the tears with my handkerchief, I
realised that the sun had warmed my body to a normal temperature again.

On the way back I tried to imagine what life had been
like in such a camp, wondering if I could have survived it,
but one could only guess at that.

The return journey went much quicker. I tried to com-
pose myself as I approached the house because I didn't
want anyone to see how I was feeling. I didn't want them
to notice what was going on inside me, how awful I felt.
Always the same mask, whatever the circumstances.

Nobody asked any questions when I came in and I was
grateful, because I wouldn't have been able to talk about
it. Thea brought me a hot cup of coffee, which revived me
somewhat. After a second cup I got up; I suddenly couldn't
bear to be in the house any longer and had to go out into
the open air. Corrie wisely stayed in the background; she
knew it would be better to leave me to myself.

I was looking for solitude, I needed to be alone with
my thoughts for a while. Nobody mentioned it; they
understood.

Fortunately we had to go home the next day because it
was Yom Kippur in two days' time and I had to be at the
synagogue all day.

The whole way home we didn't say a word about my
visit to the camp. I still couldn't talk about it.

Back at home, day-to-day life took up all my attention again, and that was just as well because the images from the camp preoccupied me far too much. I went to bed early every evening; I was mentally exhausted. During the first hours of the night I would be completely out of it, only to wake with a start at three in the morning. The first thing I would ask myself was if I had dreamed it. If I'd really gone there. Then I would realise that I really had. How often did the people who spent long months there wake up at night in a panic?

On Tuesday evening, 15 October 1985, fasting started at quarter to six and finished at quarter to seven the following evening. Like every year, the day demanded spiritual preparation. On top of that, I had been asked to blow the shofar, the ram's horn, at the end of the day, signifying that the fast of the Day of Atonement had ended. It was a great honour for me each year, only this time I hadn't practised. If it didn't go well, you couldn't just say you'd try again.

That Tuesday I came home early in the afternoon because I had to make sure I'd eaten my dinner by quarter to six. I began to lay out everything I needed to take with me: my prayer shawl, the shofar and my books. I approached this Day of Atonement with very different feelings to other years. I was almost glad that I wasn't allowed to eat or drink anything for the next twenty-five hours. I was so preoccupied with the people in the camps, how often they had been forced to fast without any prospect of a meal, like we had.

The synagogue was packed. There were also many non-Jews present on this Yom Kippur Eve. The service, which took three hours, went by quickly, and I knew that for me this fast would be very different from all others. All my thoughts were over there, in that cold, bleak camp in Bergen-Belsen.

That evening I couldn't sleep. I lay there for a while looking around, wondering if it was right for me to lie so comfortably in this king-size bed. In my mind's eye I once again saw all those nameless people in all those graves. Like me, they'd never understood what it was all for and why they'd had to go through it. Who had made the selection? Who had decided: them, but not me? No one will ever be able to give an answer, however much we want one.

The next morning I was back in the synagogue by nine o'clock in order to prepare for the service with nine other men. It got busier as the day went on, as most people came for a few hours and then went home again for a while. But a quorum of ten men was present throughout.

At five o'clock the synagogue began to gradually fill to capacity, because the closing of the fast is a very important moment for everyone. The prayers, chanted by the chazzan, the cantor, became more insistent and gradually changed into supplications. Everyone furtively glanced at the clock, because the second book of Moses, Shemot, had to be finished by quarter to seven. I was watching the clock as well because in a moment I would have to get up from the bench to take my place for the blowing of the shofar.

As I stood there and heard the chazzan recite the Shema seven times, expressing absolute belief in God, my tears started to stream down again. My feelings were a jumble of remorse, regret and sorrow, and the closer we came to the end of this Yom Kippur, the more I began to tremble.

Then the moment came for me to step up to the bimah and turn to the open ark with the Torah scrolls. I pulled my prayer shawl around my face because no one needed to see my wet cheeks.

The chazzan was reciting the closing prayer, but I could no longer follow the text through my tears. I stared rigidly at the Torah scrolls, and very slowly they disappeared from view and were replaced by many blurred faces. I recognised my parents and my brothers and my uncles, aunts and cousins, whom I had sorted through so neatly after my visit to the NIOD.

I lifted my shofar, slowly put it to my lips and took a few very deep breaths. Then the moment came. I started to blow. I began very low and quiet and then little by little let the sound swell, clean and pure, culminating in the highest note, which came like a long, slow howl.

Never had I been able to produce such a sound. It was as if I were crying out. This time the sound came not from my shofar, but straight from my heart. I sent it out beyond the walls of the synagogue, to resound from camp to camp.

I could feel the eyes of the people in the benches resting on me, because in other years I would put the shofar down when I was done and go back to my seat. Now everything was different. I stood for a moment staring into space and then slowly came back to earth. I put the shofar down and returned to my seat. Empty.

That year it felt extra special for me to celebrate the end of the fast with a wonderful meal. My children – I have always regarded my son-in-law as my child – and my grandchildren were there, six people in all. It might be sad that I can seat all my relatives around a table for six when I used to have such a big family. But I am nevertheless grateful and happy with what I've got. I need, and want, to learn to live with the living and let the dead rest in peace.

Lex with his daughter and granddaughters. (Courtesy of Fiety Lesgever)

A Word of Thanks

I want to thank all the dear people who helped me during those terrible times, but my deepest gratitude goes to Bertus, who took me out of Amsterdam and thereby gave me a second chance, a chance to live. Without him I wouldn't be here now and could never have told this story. Sadly Bertus did not live to see the end of the war; he was summarily executed by the Germans on an evil day.

My special thanks also go to my son-in-law Bernard Glaser, who didn't live to see the publication of this book. He would have been immensely proud that the publication of my story, however daunting I found it, has become a reality after all.

Besides them, I am grateful to many more people for how they helped me through the most dreadful years of my life. I would very much like to meet them all again, but that's impossible, because although they were real, their names were not.

Lex Lesgever

Acknowledgements

I would like to thank Mike Hammerstone for technical help with the images and Margaret May for her support and encouragement.

Babette Lichtenstein